394

SIMPLE FOOD FOR THE GOOD LIFE
An Alternative Cookbook

Books by Helen Nearing

THE GOOD LIFE PICTURE ALBUM

With Scott Nearing

THE MAPLE SUGAR BOOK

LIVING THE GOOD LIFE

USA TODAY

SOCIALISTS AROUND THE WORLD

BUILDING & USING OUR SUN-HEATED GREENHOUSE

CONTINUING THE GOOD LIFE

An Alternative Cookbook

SIMPLE FOOD FOR THE GOOD LIFE

A thriftie Table and the wholesom'st cheare,
All sorts of graine, of fruits a several dish:
Good Breakefasts, Dinners, Suppers, after-meales,
The hearbe for Sallads, and the hearbe that heales.
If all these things thou wants't, no further look.
All this, and more than this, lyes in this Booke.

SIR JOHN HARYNGTON,
The Schoole of Salerne, 1607

by Helen Nearing

DELACORTE PRESS/ELEANOR FRIEDE

Published by
Delacorte Press/Eleanor Friede
1 Dag Hammarskjold Plaza
New York, N.Y. 10017

ACKNOWLEDGMENTS

Excerpts from *Cookery Crockery* by Herbert M. Shelton used by permission of the author.

Excerpts from "I Can't Abear" by Walter de la Mare used by permission of the Literary Trustees of Walter de la Mare and The Society of Authors as their representative.

Excerpt from article by Mimi Sheraton used by permission of the author. First published in *Diversion* magazine (February 1974).

Excerpt from "What's in This Stuff" by Roy Andries de Groot used by permission of the author. First published in *Esquire* magazine (June 1974).

Lines from "Feast" by Edna St. Vincent Millay from COLLECTED POEMS, Harper & Row. Copyright 1923, 1951 by Edna St. Vincent Millay and Norma Millay Ellis.

Manufactured in the United States of America
First printing
Designed by MaryJane DiMassi

LIBRARY OF CONGRESS CATALOGING IN PUBLICATION DATA

Nearing, Helen.
Simple food for the good life.

Includes index.
1. Cookery (Natural foods)   2. Vegetarian cookery.
I. Title.
TX741.N4   641.5′637   80–17130
ISBN 0–440–08479–2

DEDICATION

To the Good People, Young and Old, Abroad and at Home,
who tasted, tucked in and consumed my Fodder through the
Years, and asked for Recipes, which I rarely had,
and finally persuaded me there was a Place
among the thousands of Cookbooks throughout the World
for one as idiosyncratic as this.

I SEEKE not after vayne glorie, but rather how to benefite and profite my countrie men. The good and vertuous cook, writer or reader, whose purpose is the health of the many and their owne selves will not mistake this my enterprise, which to this purpose specially tendeth, that even the meanest and most poverty-stricken of my countrie men, whose skill is not so profounde, may yet in time of their necessities have some helpes from this my booke.
D. REMBERT DODOENS,
A Nievve Herball, 1578

Wherein (friendly Reader) thou shalt finde that my whole drift is to helpe the needfull in his most want and extremity. If thou shalt finde benefit, thinke mine houres not ill wasted; if thou shalt not have occasion to approve them, yet give them thy gentle passage to others and thinke me as I am, thy Friend.
GERVASE MARKAM, *The Way to Get Wealth,*
Cheape & Good Husbandry, 1616

The meaning of publishing this is to instruct those who may not have had the opportunity of observing or collecting so much as I have done, and not in any way pretending to inform those who are full of Knowledge already.
R. BRADLEY,
The Country Housewife, 1732

This Collection of Receipts for dressing all Sorts of Kitchen Stuff, so as to afford a great Variety of cheap, healthful, and palatable Dishes, is designed for the Use of all who would live Cheap and preserve their Health to old Age; particularly for Farmers and Tradesmen in the Country, who have but small Pieces of Garden Ground and are willing to make the most of it.
ANONYMOUS,
Adam's Luxury and Eve's Cookery, 1744

Being tolerable advanced in age, and consequently in experience, I am so often consulted by young ladies about to marry, or by those who have plunged into the intricacies of domestic management, for some rules and regulations, that I have consented, if my rheumatism do not interrupt, to arrange a few pages on my own simple plan, and which I heartily recommend to all the young brides of the nation, that each may secure love and harmony in her own dear home.
MARTHA CAREFUL,
Household Hints to Young Housewives, 1853

Contents

Note to the Reader

*B*EFORE proceeding to the book proper I should doubtless say a word about my perhaps excessive use of ancient quotations. It has been my pleasure and opportunity for years to read in the rare book rooms of New York, Boston and Philadelphia libraries, and my delight has been to rescue wise and well-said words from the obscurity of library shelves.

"There are some people," says H.L. Mencken, "who read too much: the bibliobibuli. I know some who are constantly drunk on books, as other men are drunk on whiskey or religion."

I am a library inebriate; I get drunk on pithy quotations. If someone else has said it better, and earlier, why not make these sources available to you, gentle reader? Why not use their choice expressions instead of my own bald words?

I make no further excuses for sharing with you my

prized collection from other authors' works, which I lapped up avidly and found so delicious.

I collected them for no other End, than a little to divert the Reader, and to informe him of what divers Authors have writ: who have applied themselves to this Kind of Learning.

DR. M.L. LEMERY,
A Treatise of All Sorts of Foods, 1745

I want to show how delightful the old cookery book is as a book to read, not merely to keep handy on the kitchen dresser.

ELIZABETH ROBBINS PENNELL,
My Cookery Books, 1903

I quote a good deal in my talks. I like to call upon my radiant clouds of witnesses to back me up, saying the thing I would say, and saying it so much more eloquently.   LEONORA SPEYER,
On the Teaching of Poetry, 1946

(One concession I make for those who cannot accommodate to so many erudite additions in a simple cookbook. The full pages of quotations facing the chapter headings will be put in the smallest of types so that he who runs need not read. Some readers, though, will agree with me that the quotations are the best part of the book.)

Part One

SIMPLE FOOD FOR SIMPLE PEOPLE

I believe I have attempted a Branch of Cookery which Nobody has yet thought worth their while to write upon. Should I be so happy as to gain the good Opinion of my own Sex I desire no more, that will be a full Recompence for all my Trouble. If I have not wrote in the high, polite Stile, I hope I shall be forgiven; for my Intention is to instruct the lower Sort, and therefore must Treat them in their own Way. The great Cooks have such a high Way of expressing themselves that the poor Girls are at a Loss to know what they mean.   HANNAH GLASSE,
The Art of Cookery Made Plain & Easy, 1747

*H*AVING out of mine owne particular experience at Length obtained a prety volume of experimentall observations; And not knowing the length of my dayes, nay, assuredly knowing that they are drawing to their periode, I am willing to unfolde my Napkin and to deliver my poore talent abroad to the profit of some and to the pleasuring of others.

SIR HUGH PLATT,
Floraes Paradise, 1608

I have presumed to advance and set forward a Work so generally beneficial, especially to those of the meaner rank, by a cheap, profitable and easie way of providing for and maintaining of their Families. For the better and more easie effecting whereof, I have, in this small Treatise, published such as whereby every man, in the greatest times of Dearth and Scarcity, may have excellent, good and wholesome Bread and other kinds of Food for their Families, at as cheap Rates as now in times of Plenty. JOHN FORSTER,
England's Happiness Increased, 1664

Having had a Liberal Education, and many Opportunities to Improve what my younger years were Seasoned with, I have been no ways Neglectful to myself, or others, in Gaining Knowledge and Experience in such Useful things, as not only already have, but further will, prove Advantagious to both; and much oblige Posterity, which I am resting in a Silent Grave, by a Seasonable Publication of them. For since Age grows fast upon me, it is but Necessary I should do all the Good I can, before I go out of this World, that I may find the Comfort of it in another. ANONYMOUS,
The Whole Duty of a Woman, 1695

It is with diffidence that I come before the public as an Authoress. The improvement of the rising generation of Females in our Country was the motive which prompted me to this undertaking. It is not so much for the Lady of fashion and fortune as for those in the more humble walks of life. If this treatise should tend in any way to guide the inexperienced Female in the Art of Cooking, and relieve them from that embarrassment which they must otherwise experience it would be an ample compensation for this undertaking. LUCY EMERSON,
The New-England Cookery, 1808

2

1

How & Why I Came to Write about Food & Cookery

*T*HE suggestion for me, a far-from-enthusiastic and qualified cook, to write a cookbook originated years ago in France, of all places—that headquarters of chefs, epicures and gourmets. I, who spend as little time as possible at the stove and in the kitchen, who resort to few recipes or cookbooks, who throw odds and ends together for a fast meal, and who use the simplest of ingredients and procedures—to be asked to write a cookbook.

Everyone (young, old, female or male) has been flattered after putting a specially good dish on the table when guests exclaim: "What a soup! What a cook! Will you share your recipe with me? You should write a cookbook!" This trivial triumph has happened even to me.

It has been said (and probably by a good cook) that there are two kinds of people in the world: those who are good cooks and those who wish they were good cooks. I hold there is a third category: those who are not good cooks and who couldn't care less. I am happily one of

3

those, so where do I get the nerve to write a cookbook? It happened this way.

Scott and I were spending some time in the south of France, on the Mediterranean, in 1970, brushing up our French during the winter. We had a small kitchenette apartment with a balcony overlooking the bay at Ville-franche. We invited acquaintances of many nationalities in for meals. Our foreign visitors oh'd and ah'd at the soups (just vegetables of the region), the salads (perhaps more of a mixture than their usual tossed greens), the wheat berries I served them, the desserts (often mixtures of scraped apples and rolled oats, raisins, honey and lemon juice). "What's so special about that?" I snorted. "It's just a bit of this and that which happened to be available and handy. It's the simplest of foods; I'm no cook." "But tell us how you make it all. You must write a cookbook and go into all the interesting details. Everything is so unusual."

Well, perhaps—to our new French, South African, Moroccan, Japanese and Indian friends. Then I remembered a Frenchman and his wife who had eaten an extremely simple meal with us twenty or so years before, in our Vermont kitchen. The suave and elegant gentleman had enthused over a quickly thrown-together concoction. Wiping his lips, he said to his still more elegant wife, "My dear, you must get the recipe of this delicious dish." It was merely wheat berries, which he had never seen or tasted before, baked, and sweetened with maple syrup and raisins. I could hardly have served them more simply, unless our guests had been asked to chew the wheat seed raw, which has also happened.

Why do you not write and publish a Cookery-Book, was a question continually put to me. For a considerable time this scientific

4

word caused a thrill of horror to pervade my frame. . . . But you must acknowledge, respected readers, how changeable and uncertain are our feeble ideas through life. I have been drawn into a thousand gastronomic reflections, which have involved me in the necessity of deviating entirely from my former opinion, and have induced me to bring before the public the present volume, throughout which I have closely followed the plain rules of simplicity, so that every receipt cannot only clearly be understood, but easily executed. ALEXIS SOYER,
The Gastronomic Regenerator, 1846

In offering to the public the work I now produce, I have only put in order materials I had collected long ago. The occupation has been an amusing one, which I reserved for my old age.

BRILLAT-SAVARIN,
La Physiologie du Gout, 1820

The reasons which induced me to this labour were these: first to give satisfaction to the friends and favourers of my cooking; Then to give ease and light burthen to my owne heavy and full memory, so as to write down these my Receipts (adventures into Cookery). And lastly because I wished something of ease and betterment and lesse price to be available and to satisfie those younger women of this generation. GERVASE MARKHAM,
Countrey Contentments, 1613

So the French were the straws to break this camel's back and persuade me to put down in writing my rather random cooking practices. And a camel's back it was, because I have had the temerity and application to go through literally thousands of cookbooks, ancient and modern, to see what other people have written, and to see what not to bother to write. In one library alone (at Fifth Avenue and Forty-second Street in New York City) I found close to 14,000 cookbook titles, filling nine filing drawers. Fascinated, I started with manuscripts on parchment. A treatise on food by Apicius was printed on vellum in the third century. Another vellum roll called

The Form of Cury [cookery] contained 196 recipes written in the fourteenth century, in the reign of Richard II and published by a Dr. Pegge in 1780. The directions were to enable one "to make common pottages and common meats for the household as they should be made, craftily and wholesomely."

I often tackled sixty books a day, though not looking for recipes. I was interested in the format, the style, the pleasant discursiveness of the authors.

Just as the bee collects her sweets, from every flower and shrub she meets, So what from various books I drew, I give, though not the whole as new.   H.L. BARNUM,
Family Receipts, 1831

I did not presume to offer any observations of my own till I had read all that I could find written on the subject, and submitted (with no small pains) to a patient and attentive consideration of every preceding work relating to culinary concerns, that I could meet with. These books vary very little from each other, except in the prefaces. During the Herculean labour of my tedious progress through these books I have perused not fewer than two hundred and fifty of these volumes.   DR. WILLIAM KITCHINER,
The Cook's Oracle, 1817

If we read cookery books (an amusing and virtuous occupation) of all ages we find that the old ones are more interesting than useful; but they throw a light on the modes and manners of a period, and help us to visualize life in those bygone days. As for the recipes themselves, their main interest, as a rule, is not of a culinary nature as far as we are concerned. We must consider them as curious museum pieces. The proportions were enormous, the indications extravagant, the mixture of flavours alarming, and the grossness unbelievable.   X. MARCEL BOULESTIN,
The Finer Cooking, 1937

As I looked through the hundreds of old-time cookbooks I ignored "potage of stewed Boar," "roasted Conies," "baked Venison Tarte," "a dozen Quayles," "a dish of Larkes or Peacocke," and "Hogges puddings," all elaborate contrivances. Being a vegetarian, I skipped over all the poultry pages, the fish and meat, the hashes, the roasts. Being a health-foodist, I could disregard all recipes for pastas, pizzas, rissoles, fritters, pickles, canapés, doughnuts, dumplings, rolls, buns, crackers, cakes, cookies, pies, candies, jellies. I was on the trail of simpler and healthier prey. My aim was not how good does it taste, but how well does it nourish.

In the New York Public Library and in Philadelphia and in Boston I went through every book on cookery up to the 1920s. In 1921 a famous French chef, George-Auguste Escoffier, published *Le Guide Culinaire,* a volume of 2,973 recipes, and I stopped with that.

Everyone who ever wrote a cookbook (and multitudes have tried it) thinks or wishes his or hers was the cookbook to end all cookbooks. I hope the same for this book. In fact, I wish the cookbook before this one had been the last cookbook. I would have been saved a lot of time and trouble.

Mrs. A.D.T. Whitney, in her 1879 *Key to Cook-Books,* probably had the right idea. "The literature of cookery is already enormous," she wrote. "The number of receipt books is legion. I do not madly propose to add as such to the number." Yet here am I, doing that very thing. I should know better, which reminds me of the two Victorian ladies who met together over tea to consider approaching authorship.

"Write a cookbook! Don't do it, Kate! We have a perfect library of cookbooks already and of making them there appears to be no end. It requires an ordinary lifetime almost to even glance at the thousands and tens of thousands of recipes our numberless cookbooks contain. Don't do it!"

"Cousin Emmeline, you fail to comprehend my purpose. I'm not going to add another to the list of abominations miscalled cookbooks. In *my* cookbook I will deal with the essential articles of food, omitting those non-essential and indigestible messes and mixtures that have been heretofore thrust so prominently forward."
EMMA P. EWING,
Cooking and Castle-Building, 1890

Granted, there are too many cookbooks in the world and too many cooks and too much cooked food. If I cannot write a book with an entirely different attitude to food and a different slant than any other cookbook I have come across, I should stop right here. But I do aim, and hope, to make this one different. The diet I will recommend and describe will be hearty, harmless food, simple and sustaining: simple food for simple-living people, not complicated food for complex sophisticates. My aim is simplicity and economy in dressing and preparing foods. If a recipe cannot be written on the face of a 3×5 card, off with its head. The theme of my book will be: live hard not soft; eat hard not soft; seek fiber in foods and in life.

The Author has not here undertaken to cook out an Art of Gluttony, or to teach the Rich and Lazy how to grow fatter.
PATRICK LAMB,
Royal Cookery: or The Compleat Court-Cook, 1726

This work is not designed to spread a taste for pernicious luxuries.
A Boston Housekeeper,
The Cook's Own Book, 1854

I do not write "to please the popular palate," as Edmund Burke wrote in 1770, in his *Thoughts on the Cause of the Present Discontents.* This book is to be written by a simple woman who doesn't read or use recipes, who doesn't set a fancy table. It is to be for simple-living people who have other things paramount on their minds rather than culinary concerns, than eating and preparing dainty and elaborate dishes. It is not for those who are interested in eating as such. This is for those frugal, abstemious folk who eat to nourish their bodies and leave self-indulgent delicacies to the gourmets.

I have a sister who was a born cook. She moves in carriage trade circles and delights and surpasses in whipping up elaborate dishes out of her head. She could write an excellent cookbook, but she's too busy playing golf. *Fancy Food for Fancy Folk,* she could call it. I am the simple-minded sister, whose book details simple food for simple people.

To some people food is the most interesting, exciting and engrossing subject in their lives. They are food addicts. To others it is a very marginal matter. Count me as one of those, although I can at times enjoy something good to eat, along with anyone else. Why should I condemn what is beautiful or delicious amongst the marvelous creations of earth? I only say: go easy; be aware of the highest priorities.

A man should be ashamed to take his food if he has not alchemy enough in his stomach to turn some of it into intense and enjoyable occupation. ROBERT LOUIS STEVENSON,
Men and Books, 1888

Many people rail against attributing much importance to the pleasures of the table; but it is not observable that these moralists are more averse than others to gratification of the palate when opportunity occurs. It is a poor philosophy whose object is to decrease the means of pleasure and enjoyment.

LOUIS EUSTACHE UDE,
The French Cook Book, 1828

Cookbooks are usually designed for people who are overfed and oversupplied with food and who are looking for tasty additions to stimulate their worn-out appetites. Overeating on overcooked food is an acquired habit, much like smoking and drinking—an indulgence rather than a physiological need. I like crisp, hard, crunchy foods, raw if possible, which you have to chew—not soft, soggy, slip-go-downs.

> Every kind of food should be so left by cookery as to task to their fullest reasonable extent the masticatory organs—the teeth. And yet, is it not correct to say that three-fourths of the effort spent in what is called cookery, has a tendency to encourage the teeth in indolence? WILLIAM A. ALCOTT, *The Young Wife*, 1838

The food I prepare and serve is meant to build healthy bodies, not to cater to corrupted taste buds that urge one to eat unhealthy things long after the claims of hunger have been satisfied. Enough is as good as a feast: better, in fact, because if you don't overeat, you don't get sick or fat.

The more appetizing foods are made, the more is eaten and the worse for the health of the body. If you wish to grow thinner, diminish your dinner, someone has said. If you eat twice as much popcorn when it is heavily buttered and salted, why butter and salt it? Eat a moderate amount of plain popcorn and then stop. If you are not hungry enough to eat unsalted popcorn, or bread without loads of butter and jam, or salad without a spicy dressing or sauce, why eat at all? Why not wait until you are hungry, without craving extra stimulants? If salt and seasoning makes you eat more of a food—leave off the salt and seasoning and eat less of a food. It's as simple as that.

Men dig their Graves with their own Teeth and die more by
those fatal Instruments than the Weapons of their Enemies.

THOMAS MOFFETT,
Helth's Improvement, 1600

Unhappye are they whyche have more appetite than thyr sto-
make.   SIR THOMAS ELYOT,
The Bankette of Sapience, 1545

Food is fuel for the body. Don't overoctane or over-
load your engine. Give it the right food, easy to digest.
And don't flood it (the stomach being the carburetor), or
the engine won't work. It will backfire or refuse to start
at all.

To get back to my French friends: I told them: "I'm
not a cook. I don't like to cook. I cook only when it is
necessary, and then no animal carcasses, remember. I'm
a birthright vegetarian and wouldn't touch dead flesh
with a pole, let alone cook and consume it. What kind of
a book would that make?" "Ah, but that's just what is
needed: a guide for the unenlightened, taste-corrupted
cooks. Do a 'Why I Don't Cook Book'; a 'Cook No More
Book'; an 'Anti-Cook Book.' "

The question of my writing such a book came up again
and again, in various forms, in various countries, and
even at home in our own kitchen. Eating our simple fare,
friends and strangers alike quite often said, "Tell me
what went into this outlandish dish. May we have the
recipe? I want to try it out for myself. You ought to write
a cookbook."

So, gradually, the odd idea filtered through to me.
Maybe I *should* try to get down on paper some of our
ways of eating: our "Horse Chow," our "Carrot Croak-
ers," "Scott's Emulsion" and "Bishop Brown's Mucilage." Was it possible they might be of sufficient worth
to interest the general public? Was I good enough?

11

Asked what he thought of a certain cook, a man pondered, then came out with "More interesting than good." Now that's more my line: my cooking may be interesting, but I don't pretend to be good, unless, as Joseph Conrad wrote in the preface to his wife's cookbook (JESSIE CONRAD, *A Handful of Cookery for a Small House*, 1923): "By good cooking I mean the conscientious preparation of the simple food of everyday life, not the more or less skillful concoction of idle feasts and rare dishes."

Most of my throwing things together is experimental —just as all cooking originally was experimental. Necessity need not be the mother of invention, but it often is in cooking. I like to have a dearth of materials out of which to make things, not an overflowing refrigerator and pantry. It fosters more ingenuity.

A one-time brainstorm like the following is very elementary improvisation, made up on the spur of the moment. I needed something quick to feed Scott for supper. It was a hot evening, and I didn't want to build a fire. I took a bowl of cooked wild rice (a rich gift from a rich friend) and mixed it with some leftover cooked celery from the day before. I opened a can of pitted black olives (another gift; I do not usually stock such delicacies), drained them of juice and threw them into the rice. Scott had left a few handfuls of red and white radishes at the door for salad. I cut them up and added them to the rice for dash and color. A swish of olive oil, a scatter of sea and celery salt, and the lot turned into an extremely edible, simple, cold dish—but hardly notable enough for a cookbook.

Unless for purposes of research, as in preparing for this book, I rarely read or consult a cookbook. I don't look inside a cookbook six times a year. I have many of them,

12

but rarely use them. I'm a spur-of-the-moment cook and make do with what materials are at hand in pantry, cellar or garden, and let my mind and fingers work on them. Something usually emerges which is edible and nutritious. Mine is a rough and ready cookery.

> Know on thyself thy genius must depend. All books of cookery, all helps of art, All critic learning, all commenting notes, are vain if void of genius thou wouldst cook.
>
> DIONYSIUS THE CARTHUSIAN, 1450

Someone gave me, back in the 1930s, Adelle Davis's *Let's Cook It Right*. One page and one alone has been used and smudged with finger marks: the rose hip recipes. When moving to Maine we found great patches of Rugosa roses growing by the shore. I knew they were supposed to be full of vitamin C, but I had no idea how to prepare them. Her recipes helped me work out a way of my own. When I wrote Adele about the one grimy page, she was pleased, as she had thought no one would go as far as to be interested in preserving rose hips.

I do not cook by a book and do not expect you to. You need never use a cookbook. Nobody taught me how to cook and nobody need teach you. You can do as I did and teach yourself.

My mother, although she was Dutch and might have been brought up as a good housekeeper, was no cook. She barely knew the kitchen in the large mansion back of the Rijks Museum in Amsterdam where her uncle (her foster-father) was director. At home in New Jersey I remember as a child a succession of Kates and Berthas and Maggies who tended to household affairs. My father (with a European background which led him never to enter the kitchen) and I (always practicing my violin when work had to be done, or so my sister says), accepted food on the table as a natural occurrence and right. The extent of my cooking capacity till my mid-twenties was making popovers as a teen-ager for the family's Sunday breakfast. And that was a spontaneous and gratuitous contribution, as I liked the peace and quiet of early Sunday mornings before anyone else was up. Otherwise, I kept my violinistic hands out of kitchen work. Like many in my spoiled generation in America in the first quarter century, I avoided household chores, and when I became responsible for a household of my own I had little or no experience.

Under every possible disadvantage of ignorance, inexperience, and lack of proper materials, I started not from zero but from frozen depths of ignorance which no thermometer records.
SHEILA KAYE-SMITH,
Kitchen Fugue, 1945

It is said that good cooks are born, not made. I was not born a good cook; I did not become one, and I am not one now, but I can feed a large family or dozens of visitors quickly, easily, substantially and economically at the drop of a hat. Six more for lunch, I see, as a car drives up and piles out strangers when we are just sitting down to eat. Add water, tomatoes, onions and parsley to the soup. Put some buckwheat groats on to cook for five minutes. If we're eating salad, add some stalks of celery, some green peppers and knife up an extra head of lettuce. Bring more apples or applesauce from the cellar for a dessert. A dozen unexpected people can sit down to eat an abundant meal in twenty minutes: nothing fancy, but everyone gets filled. There is always enough and to spare. No one need go hungry. Cervantes says, in

Don Quixote, "In a house where there is plenty, supper is soon cooked."

In the contrivance of these my labours, I have so managed them for the general good, that those whose Purses cannot reach to the cost of rich Dishes, I have descended to their meaner Expences, that they may give, though upon a sudden Treatment, to their Kindred, Friends, Allies and Acquaintance, a handsome and relishing entertainment in all seasons of the year, though at some distance from Towns or Villages.   ROBERT MAY,
The Accomplisht Cook, 1685

I staunchly determined, and tried to stick to it, that any recipes included in my book would be straight from the garden where possible, cooked slightly if at all, at low temperatures to kill fewer vitamins and enzymes, with little added flavoring and the fewest possible dishes, pans and utensils used. The simpler the food, the better, I think; the rawer, the better; the fewer mixtures, the better. This way of eating involves less preparation, less cooking, easier digestion, more food value, better health, and more money saved.

So, the objective of this book will be: to write on simple food for simple-living people; to pass on to the New World young Americans who are leaving civilized society in droves, ways to sustain and nourish themselves which call for little experience, little time, little money, few ingredients and a minimum of complication.

The means by which the Author has sought to work out his design, will, it is hoped, be found to combine entertainment with utility, and amusement with practical information.
JOHN TIMBS,
Hints for the Table, 1859

15

T WAS the Night before Christmas, or so sayeth the Book.
Not a Creature was stirring, excepting the Cook.

ANONYMOUS, Dateless

Though husbandrie seemeth to bring in the gaines,
Yet huswiferie labours seeme equal in paines.
Some respite to husbands the weather may send,
But huswives' affairs have never an end.
Wash dishes, lay leavens, save fire, and away,
Lock doors and to bed, a good huswife will say.

THOMAS TUSSER,
Five Hundreth Pointes of Good Husbandrie, 1557

Look you, I keep his house, and I wash, wring, brew, bake, scour, dress and
drink, make the beds, and do all myself. 'Tis a great charge to come under one
body's hand.
MRS. CLARISSA PACKARD,
Recollections of a Housekeeper, 1834

The treadmill routine of the week is: washing, baking, ironing, fixing dried
fruit, airing clothes, sewing, cleaning, baking and cleaning again. So it goes
week after week. Eating and drinking, cooking and cleaning, scrubbing and
scouring we go through life; and only lay down our implements at the verge
of the grave! . . . You bake, and boil, and fry, and stew; worry and toil, just as
if people's principle business in this world was to learn how much they could
eat—and eat it.
JANE G. SWISSHOLM,
Letters to Country Girls, 1853

All nice cooking—be its materials ever so simple—is more or less troublesome.

LADY BARKER,
First Lessons in the Principles of Cooking, 1874

The most conventional customs cling to the table. Farmers who wouldn't
drive a horse too hard expect pie three times a day.   ELLA H. RICHARDS,
The Healthful Farmhouse, 1906

Even though I love cooking, I do not want to spend endless hours in the
preparation process.
ALAN HOOKER,
Vegetarian Gourmet Cooking, 1970

16

2

The Work of Cooking: Need It Be Drudgery?

*T*HERE is an old Scotch rhyme on the drudgery of cookery: "Frae morn to e'en it's naught but toiling, at baking, roasting, frying, boiling."

My word for today, and every day, is that woman's place is *not* necessarily in the kitchen, but anywhere else she wants to be and is competent to fill a job.

If cooking be your dish, stick to it and bake and fry and broil and roast. To you it will be your pleasure and not your work; to you it will not be drudgery. I am of the other camp and begrudge time spent indoors for almost any purpose, and certainly not for fussing and filling up with food.

Mankind is said to be a cooking animal (or has become one). I am not a cooking woman. And in defense of other females who feel as I do, I hold that women need not hang over stoves and should not spend the major part of their time fooling with food and household work.

It is said that work is only work if you'd rather be doing something else. Well, I'd rather be reading (or writing) a good book, playing good music, building a wall, gardening, swimming, skating, walking—anything that is more active, more intellectual, or more inspiring. I get the tending to food over as soon as possible and out I go under the sky or to my music or books.

My aim is to reduce the fuss and bother of food-preparing to the minimum. Make a meal edible, nutritious and plentiful, set it on the table with the utmost simplicity and say to all comers: "Soup's on; come and get it." If they like it, good. If they don't, let them fill up elsewhere and otherwise. I've done what I'm going to do.

You may have heard the story of the farm woman who spent her daylight hours preparing food for half a dozen farmhands and who one afternoon went quietly crazy. As she was led to the wagon taking her to the looney house, she kept repeating: "And they ate it all in twenty minutes. They ate it all in twenty minutes." There were doubtless other ways this lady could have spent her life more happily and creatively.

William A. Alcott visited "a humble cottage" in the early 1800s and was invited to take dinner.

> There was not much preparation to be made. It was but a minute's work to set on a large dish of boiled hominy, a bowl of apples, a small vessel of molasses, a small cup of milk, and a few plates. Not a word of apology was made. It was indeed a plainer dinner than I had been accustomed to find abroad; but it was wholesome and agreeable. And then, the little labor it required!
> *The Mother in Her Family,* 1838

The same author speaks disapprovingly of the way women usually worked at household tasks in his day.

> Let him who would live on small means resort to simplicity at the same meal. Let him consider how much time and labor it costs

his wife to prepare half a dozen or a dozen sorts of food for the same meal, when a single liberal dish would be far more healthful and economical, as well as equally agreeable.

Ways of Living on Small Means, 1837

I don't mind work, hard work, but I want it to be for a more long-lived purpose and intent. William Saroyan put it succinctly: "I really don't enjoy a lot of fuss about getting a little food down the gullet and into the gut."[1] John Russell, in the fifteenth century, used more complicated words: "Cookes with their newe conceytes, choppage, and gryndynge many new curies alle day, they ar contryvynge and fyndynge that that provoke the peple to perelles passage and throu nice excesse of suche receytes, of the life to make a endynge."[2]

Why go to a lot of trouble, and use a lot of time and energy, just feeding the body? By keeping foods and meals simple and easy, the tasks may be so shortened that there is little labor involved. Keep frills and fanciness to a minimum. Keep fundamentals in the foreground. Try to get the most nourishment for the least effort. Learn what foods the body requires—the vitamins, minerals and proteins for good functioning. Find the natural right diet and stick to it.

I believe the work of feeding people could be simplified to such a point that it would take less time to prepare a meal than to eat it, whereas now it is usually the other way around. Perhaps that might be the test for rational eating. If you eat for half an hour, or an hour, put only that much (or less) time into preparation; no more. Then you would be closer to living simply on simple food.

[1]"Twenty Is the Greatest Time in Any Man's Life," *The Saturday Evening Post*, March 1977
[2]*The Boke of Nurture*, 1452

19

Eat applesauce or a raw apple instead of an apple pie amalgamation. If you're going to eat potatoes, don't go to the trouble or fuss of frying or mashing, both of which involve unnecessary work. Scrub them and bake them in the oven and eat plain, or with butter and salt. What could be more delicious or simpler for a meal? Instead of cooking rolled oats into a gluey mess, throw a cup or handful of raw oats into a bowl, add a bit of oil, lemon juice and raisins, and you'll have a chewy, unprocessed, nourishing dish ready in seconds. We call it Horse Chow.

Our pantry has barrels and cans of varied grains which can be eaten raw or cooked up with the minimum of trouble. I refuse to make anything that takes half an hour or more to concoct. Why spend a couple of hours making bread when a couple of minutes will provide as good or better nourishment for a family with plain unadulterated millet, buckwheat, or wheat seed or oats? Instead of mixing and kneading, what could be easier than pouring boiling water on millet or buckwheat groats, leaving the pot simmering on the hot stove for ten to fifteen minutes? In that small amount of time, with no further preparation, the grain is ready to eat hot or cold, with butter or oil, or with syrup or honey, or with peanut butter, or with raisins or dates, or with cut-up apples or bananas.

The elimination of baking, frying, broiling, also does away with the endless cleaning up and scrubbing of pots and pans. Eat with one dish or bowl. Eliminate all nonessentials in tools and utensils as well as elaboration in food preparation.

Nutritional value should come before taste value; so should economy and ease of preparation. Our menus are simple, but vary within the daily pattern; some fruit or fruit juice and our own herb tea for breakfast; a hearty

vegetable soup, with boiled grains, peanut butter, honey and apples for lunch; a big salad, some cooked vegetable from the garden and a fruit dessert for supper. Every day the soup can be different. The grain can be millet, buckwheat, oats, wheat or rye. The salad need never be the same. The vegetables vary with the season. Our dessert can be any of many fruits, raw or cooked. But the general pattern remains, so that the diet is uninvolved and the preparation uncomplicated.

If I were put to it to set down a schedule of our eating habits I would say we try to stick as close as possible to the following regime: 35 percent fruit, 50 percent vegetable (with one-third green leafy, one-third yellow, and one-third juicy); 10 percent protein, and 5 percent fat. This is not rigid, of course, but is our aim.

Scott is the easiest man in the world to feed—as long as I keep the fare simple. Hand him a compounded, mixed-up conglomerate over which I may have spent some time, and he will ask plaintively, "No baked potatoes today?" Both he and I would be content with a green salad and a baked potato every night for supper all year round. Why trouble oneself or one's stomach with more? Although I will admit that seemed to be carried to extremes on one occasion.

We were staying with a Japanese family in Tokyo for some days. The timid though eager housewife asked what we usually ate, so that she could prepare the first evening meal. I said, "Oh, just a salad and a baked potato," hoping that would be the simplest meal for her, as it would have been for me. The dear soul gave us salad and baked potatoes for every meal while we were there! One could feed far worse, and it did us no harm, but she was left with a curious idea of the American diet.

Thoreau might have been an even easier guest. At a

table, when asked by Emerson which dish he preferred, he replied nonchalantly, "The nearest." Richard Burton, author of the 1628 book *The Anatomy of Melancholy*, went even further in unconcern than Thoreau, in the following salty language: "What care I of what stuff my excrements are made?"

If I lived alone and in a warm part of the world instead of New England, I would subsist on fruits and nuts and succulent raw green vegetables. As we live in a cold climate where fruits and nuts do not abound, I cook more or less, and the less the better. We were lucky in one way when we moved from Vermont to Maine. We left a superb baking stove in Vermont and bought (sight unseen) an elegant white enameled Home Comfort stove, the best supposedly on the market at that time, with the largest firebox. It was beautifully insulated for a centrally heated house (which ours was not), and it wouldn't heat and it wouldn't bake. So from then on I did little baking and mostly cooked top-of-the-stove. My cooking was lessened, perforce.

Simplify, simplify, as Thoreau said. Make your wants moderate and your burdens will be less. Make your feast days fast days. "On natal or your nuptial day then is a time to shun the tempting board," wrote Dr. John Armstrong.[3] On Christmas, Thanksgiving, New Year's Day, Easter, any such holiday, when housewives are toiling and overfed eaters are stuffing, Scott and I give a vacation to the stomach and to the cook by going without any solid food, just drinking water or juices. We do it as a protest against the folly of feasting, against the national gluttony of overfed people overeating, and in compassion to the overworked digestive system, and to the

[3]*The Art of Preserving Health*, 1804

22

cook. It is a good rest for the stomach as well as for the housewife. Also, one day a week (usually Sunday) we fast. No cooking. And for breakfast year-round I cook nothing. Often in the spring, for a good spring inner-cleaning, we go on an apple diet for ten days or so. We eat all the raw apples we want and can hold. It is not like a total fast when one's energies may become depleted. It is a mono diet, with which one can go on working.

A diet of fruit requires less seasoning, less cooking, less labour in preparation than a diet of cereals and vegetables. . . . As civilization advances on its present lines of complexity, more and more seasonings and elaborate compounds are added to these cereals and vegetables, until in our modern cuisine and in well-ordered establishments a chef must be provided whose sole claim for employment is his ability to concoct and work up highly complex and cunningly seasoned dishes and sauces.

DR. EMMET DENSMORE,
How Nature Cures, 1892

Dear reader, do read this book in order to learn not to cook so much. Make your meals simple, simpler, simplest —quick, quicker, quickest. And in the time and energy you will save, write a poem; make music; sew a fine seam; commune with nature; play tennis; visit a friend. Keep drudgery out of your life. If you love cooking, it is not work for you or drudgery. That's fine. Go to it and enjoy the joy of cooking. But if it is drudgery, stop it, or lessen it; you will be able to eat well and then go and do your own thing.

*W*E must guard against those sorts of food which persuade us to eat when we are not hungry, bewitching the appetite. For is there not, within a temperate simplicity, a wholesome variety of eatables—vegetables, roots, olives, herbs, milk, cheese, fruits, and all kinds of dry food? For, of sorts of food, those are the most proper which are fit for immediate use without fire, since they are readiest: and second to these are those which are the simplest.

TITUS FLAVIUS CLEMENS,
The Instructor, 220 A.D.

If the human race would but listen to the voice of reason it would recognize that chefs are as superfluous as soldiers.   SENECA,
Epistle to Lucilius, 62 A.D.

Time may come when Men with Angels may participate, and find no inconvenient Diet . . . And Eve, within, due at her hour prepared for dinner savoury fruits, of taste to please true appetite . . . A while discourse they hold—no fear lest dinner cool.   JOHN MILTON,
Paradise Lost, 1665

Raw food is both more natural and more pleasant: more natural, because it is prepar'd with less toil, and being cook'd by nature itself, serves nature more adequately, to all intents and purposes. It neither entices men to eat till they be unable for their affairs, nor brings it sickness; it affords strength, and prolongs life.   SIR GEORGE MACKENZIE, *A Moral Essay,*
Preferring Solitude to Public Employment, 1685

The Delicacies and true Satisfactions of a sober Repast and the infinite Convenience of what a well-stor'd Garden affords, costing neither Fuel nor Fire to boil, Pains or Time to gather and prepare. All so near at hand, readily drest, and of so easie Digestion as neither to offend the Brain or dull the Senses.

JOHN EVELYN,
Acetaria, 1699

Taste the feast by Nature spread.
SAMUEL JOHNSON, *To Purchase Heaven,* 1760

No carving to be done, no knife to grate the tender ear and wound the stony plate.   JOEL BARLOW,
The Hasty-Pudding, 1796

24

3

To Cook or Not to Cook: Raw Versus Cooked Food

O NE way to reduce the housewife's work by half is to make raw foods a major part of the diet, or eat raw foods entirely. In warm tropical regions one could live on native fruits and nuts, picked and eaten where they grow. They are the easiest, best and most natural foods of all—unprocessed, succulent, vibrant, full of life and nourishment, with no extensive gap between the life-giving forces of the plant and the living forces of our bodies.

Food that has not been treated by heating—raw greens and raw fruits—are a better source of vitamins than any dead, altered food. They should be eaten when picked, as close to the living, growing state as possible. Nature has prepared these foods for us. The sun, air, soil, rains have all done their work, and we have the instant benefit. They are living foods—sunlight foods.

The sun is our central station of radiating energy. The warm penetrating rays of the sun ripen and cook the foods of man.

> Those slow penetrating rays that color fruits, brown and ripen
> nuts, and tint the leaves of vegetables, prepare such foods for
> ready serving. Further cooking by artificial methods tends to
> detract from their food value. — JAMES FAULKNER,
> *The Unfired Food Diet,* 1923

Fruits and nuts, with the addition of green vegetables, furnish all the food factors needed by man's organism. Raw foods keep the bloodstream clean and healthy. If young and fresh they are delectable. Celery and green peppers (two of my favorite vegetables) are unsurpassable for crisp tastiness if eaten raw. Cooked, they become a lifeless, tasteless mass. It is a great pity to put them to the fire.

There is no doubt that cooking, even conservative cooking, kills part of the life in our foods. We raise temperatures so high that the life forces are destructively altered, disintegrated or completely killed. A cooked pea can never sprout into a new plant. Cooked or canned or frozen foods are embalmed, dead foods. They may contain a few heat-resistant elements but few if any enzymes of life. Cooking is killing, incinerating. Food can be cooked to virtual death. Real death, its cremation, comes with only charred remains of life. Cook long enough and you have ashes.

The more we move toward a diet of chiefly unfired food, the healthier and more vigorous we shall become. Some prefer to use the term "unfired foods" or "living foods" instead of "raw foods." To them the word "raw" implies something crude, unfinished, immature, unripe, coarse or rough. On the contrary, a ripe raw tomato or banana is a completely finished product, perfect in itself, needs no additions, no sweetenings, no seasonings, no stimulant to appetite. The food provided by nature should be left as close as possible to the form it had when growing. Cooked food, unless flavorings, spices or sauces are added, cannot beat fresh raw food in tastiness.

The very best way to eat a fruit is straight off the tree and without doing anything to it. We shouldn't peel, slice, or chop it up; and we shouldn't cook it.
LESLEY VINE,
Ecological Eating, 1971

It seems to me that to pull an apple from a living tree or some fresh green beans from their vines and transfer them in this form to our living digestive tract is to give ourselves a plus factor that is diminished when cooking is interposed between the two acts.
DR. FRED D. MILLER,
Open Door to Health, 1971

We should eat live food, consisting of living cells. Food, even live food, injected into the body, cannot give life of itself. The living body and its vital force must work on it. Food introduced into the body of a corpse would undergo no vital change; it would gradually be decomposed along with the corpse. It is the mysterious life power or vital force that appropriates, assimilates and utilizes food. How can dead cells nourish a living body? The interchange of energies between the living cells in food substances and the tissue cells in our bodies gives unrivaled health-giving powers.

There is something in the freshness of food, especially vegetable food—some form of energy perhaps; it may be certain rays of light or electrical property—which gives to it a health-promoting influence. Certain it is that no synthetic diet that I have been able to devise has equalled in health-sustaining qualities one composed of the fresh foodstuffs as nature provides them.
SIR ROBERT MCCARRISON,
Nutrition and Natural Health, 1944

The Chinese realized that the vitality of vegetables could be destroyed by improper cooking, and they emphasized the nutritional superiority of raw or partially cooked vegetables.

DR. LEE SU JAN,
The Fine Art of Chinese Cooking, 1962

I like Chinese cooking because of the noise it makes in one's mouth—all those crisp vegetables, the sound of bean shoots being crushed, is very refreshing indeed.

Article in *Vogue* magazine, June, 1973

Let me eat young radishes and cabbages or a green pea, but no ragout, cotelette, compote, creme or any hint of cooking. For my part, I am surfeited with cookery. I cry "something raw, if you please," something that has never been touched by hand except the one that pulled it off the blooming tree or uprooted it from the honest ground.   M.E.W. SHERWOOD,
The Art of Entertaining, 1892

Man alone submits his victuals, before using them, to the art of cookery. Almost all the food the human race eats is cooked. Yet are we so smart to eat cooked food, and the monkey so stupid to eat raw food? Nature has produced foods that are as normal to man as grasses are to the herbivore or as flesh is to the carnivore. Why then do we take the trouble to cook our food? Why indeed? We have corrupted domesticated animals till they are as unhealthy as we are. Wild animals do not have the diseases of civilized man and his animal slaves. Their food is raw and unadulterated.

Animals do not sit down to a table loaded with a variety of dishes collected from every zone. They eat of one kind at a time, and therefore never over-eat. They have grass and water today, and grass and water tomorrow, and so on through their entire lives, and yet they are in perfect health.

DR. A.F. REINHOLD,
Nature Versus Drugs, 1898

Imagine feeding a baked apple to a horse instead of a crisp raw apple, or cooked oatmeal instead of raw oats. A cow or giraffe or elephant could not live on a diet of cooked grass. Would we feed braised lettuce to a rabbit? If they would eat it and become accustomed to it they would become as unhealthy as the human race.

But then the majority of the human race says we cook because the food tastes better. Does it taste better when it is cooked? Only to a palate perverted by habit and custom, as the sharp acrid taste of chewing tobacco grows on the chewer, or the betel nut tang grows on the Indian user. Does a cooked carrot taste better than a raw carrot? Only when artificially sweetened or unnaturally seasoned, if then. One does not put sauce on a raw apple. But when we bake it (kill it by cooking), to add savor we have to put on cinnamon or nutmeg, sugar or maple syrup, raisins and cream.

Mrs. Sarah Tyson Rorer, in an 1898 cookbook called *Left Overs,* says that "the object of cooking is to draw out the proper flavor of each individual ingredient used in the preparation of a dish, and render it more easy of digestion." But cooking smothers the proper flavor of each individual ingredient. And as to digestion, a bowl of young raw peas or a couple of raw peaches stimulates the digestive tract toward evacuation far more fully, quickly and easily than the same foods deadened by cooking. Try it.

I bake such solid and hard foods as potatoes and squash, though I have been known to serve raw potato slices, cut very thin, and unpeeled, as dainty hors d'oeuvres, with cream cheese and an olive atop, to visiting ladies of the local garden clubs. They crunched delightedly, with no idea that I was serving them raw

29

potatoes. Sliced Jerusalem artichokes, raw, would have done as well.

Peas in their shells I often put in a great bowl on the supper table for guests to shell for themselves. (When young and tender, we eat the shells too.) For a good summer dish I often serve cucumbers, radishes, scallions, chives, young zucchini and small tomatoes in bowls, and we eat them by hand. It is refreshing to have on the table slivers of raw carrots and celery, slices of green peppers and cauliflower flowerets.

Train yourself to like the simple, easy, healthy, uncomplicated foods, eschewing the nauseous overcooked mixtures. Try eating raw some of the things you usually cook: Yes, even grains and potatoes. I have given a handful of raw wheat seed to youngsters to chew into the most delicious chewing gum, with a delicate flavor far outdoing the boughten stuff. At first they found it gratey and pebbly in their mouths, but if they persevered in chewing the mouthful for five or ten minutes they were entranced and found it the best chewing gum ever.

We have in this country hundreds of articles of food which can be more advantageously used without cooking; yet the cook intrudes his art, bakes, boils, stews, broils, and heats these things until their original elements are wholly changed, until many of them are rendered almost totally valueless. Thus robbed of their elementary and delicious flavors, the cook endeavors to make them appeal to the sense of taste by mixing, jumbling together, spicing, and using decoctions called extracts, the properties of which he knows absolutely nothing, until the original substance is so disguised that it cannot be recognized in taste, color and flavor.   MR. & MRS. EUGENE CHRISTIAN,
Uncooked Foods and How to Use Them, 1904

Cooking and other modes of preparation are artificialities and should be handled with discretion. The greasy concoctions and

kitchen mutilations of civilization might much better be left
undone. C.C. & S.M. FURNAS,
Man, Bread and Destiny, 1937

Raw Herbs are a sublime kind of Food, and are to be preferred
before that which is boyled; for the pure Volatile Spirit in Herbs
cannot endure the violence of the fire. That lively Tincture and
spirituous part which it had whilst raw can never be retriev'd by
all the Ingredients Nature or Art can afford.
THOMAS TRYON,
The Way to Health, Long Life & Happiness, 1683

There is no substitute for the raw natural food of nature. Boiling, baking, frying, cooking, freezing, drying,
salting away, storing and generally preserving food is a
poor substitute for eating things fresh and raw.

If you must cook, aim at the shortest time possible on
the stove, and serve immediately. In your diet, aim for
at least 50 percent of all your food to be raw. Eat *some*
raw food at each meal. This will help neutralize the
damage done by cooked, deadened or poisoned foods.
Use low temperatures for cooking. Bake, or steam; use
"vapor cooking," with a very small amount of water.
Boiling is better than frying; baking is better than boiling, so is steaming; raw is best of all.

Your Herbs and Pulses should not be over-boyled, for then the
spirituous parts and balsamick body will instantly evaporate, and
your Food will become flat and heavy, losing its pure natural
Colour, Smell and Taste, and is nothing so pleasant and wholesom; it were better that it be under rather than over done,
because of the tenderness of the Green Herbs.
THOMAS TRYON,
The Way to Health, Long Life & Happiness, 1683

I have had some failures in my raw food ventures:
notably when I delivered some of my rose hip jam to an

31

epicure shop in the neighborhood. I had thickened the hard-to-stabilize mixture with grated raw potato, a trick I learned from my German grandmother. The buyer exclaimed, "This is an exquisite product. Is that grated ginger in the jam?" After I told him it was raw potato he ordered no more for his shop. I should have kept my mouth shut.

> If you perhaps wou'd try some Dish unknown, which more peculiarly you'd make your own, Like antient Sailors still regard the Coast, by ven'tring out too far you may be lost.
>
> WILLIAM KING,
> *The Art of Cookery,* 1709

I'm sure no cook is really good without a lively imagination and the will to use it. They venture sometimes beyond their depth, but come up smiling and with new recipes. Robert Tristram Coffin, the Maine poet, was part of an admiring family who had such a real cook in his mother.

> My mother worked by sight, by sound, by feel, by fancy, by sudden inspiration. The size of your family, the time of the year, the adoration of your boys—these were better guides than any cook-book. My mother never used a cook-book in her life. Her cook-book was her heart and her head and her deft hands. It was her sense of judgment and fair play, which having a large family had taught her. She cooked by philosophy and human nature. By the way a hungry man looked out of his eyes at her when he came in from work. *Mainstays of Maine,* 1944

Mrs. Coffin must have loved to cook. Another woman who apparently enjoys cooking goes by the incandescent name of Crescent Dragonwagon. She explodes in joy in *The Commune Cook-Book* (1972):

Man, I love to cook. I love to hold a vegetable in my hand, an eggplant or a carrot or an onion. I love to slice it open, hear the sound as I cut through it, note the difference between the outside and inside of it, see the beautiful patterns inside, the seeds in the eggplant, the layers of the onion, the orange star-flower pattern in a carrot. I love to beat and sift and stir and measure and pour. I love putting together all these good ingredients and watching them turn into something new.

Bravo for her! But I still deplore being preoccupied by "what shall I make for dinner tonight" to the exclusion of much else of more consequence. I would like to de-emphasize food instead of stressing it.

A lady, Prudence Smith, had almost a psychopathic interest in food when she wrote in her 1831 book on *Modern American Cookery:* "My mind is, as it were, inbued with the spirit of cookery: and I never see any animal or vegetable whatever without thinking in my own mind whether it might peradventure be wrought into some savoury dish." *I* never see an animal or vegetable but I think it should be left *out* of the cooking pot.

My good friend, Dr. Herbert M. Shelton, who has had decades of experience in serving raw foods at his health school in San Antonio, Texas, has given me permission to adapt the following points from his little-known pamphlet on *Cookery Crookery.*

The Disadvantages of Cooking

1. Cooking coagulates the proteins of milk, eggs, meat, etc., making them tough and (with the exception of egg protein) less digestible, while impairing their food values.
2. Cooking alters the fats in food, rendering them less

digestible and converting some of them into poisons.

3. Cooking causes a great loss of the soluble minerals in the food and renders it less nutritious.

4. Cooking destroys the elementary plant form, tearing down its structure, changing its composition and bringing about certain destructive changes in the element-groupings in all foods, returning a part of these elements, especially the organic salts, to their inorganic and therefore useless state, so that a large part of their mineral content is lost.

5. Cooking renders starches less digestible and more prone to fermentation.

6. Cooking destroys the vitamins in foods.

The Advantages of Raw Foods

1. Uncooked food, requiring more chewing, supplies the teeth and gums with much-needed exercise.

2. The necessary chewing insures proper salivation and therefore easier digestion.

3. Long chewing tends to prevent overeating.

4. Uncooked food preserves the teeth and stomach from the injury produced by hot foods.

5. Uncooked foods possess the proper proportion of nutritious and bulk matter.

6. Meals of one type of raw fruits or vegetables are more readily digested.

7. Uncooked foods are not so easily adulterated as are the canned, pickled, embalmed foods so largely eaten today.

8. Uncooked foods, if spoiled, cannot be camouflaged and passed off on us as good food, as cooked foods can be.

9. The uncooked diet saves time, food and labor in preparation.

It stands to reason that one should cook as little as possible, as short a time as possible, and avoid it entirely if possible. Cook nothing that can be advantageously eaten raw.

*O*H, how criminal it is for flesh to be stored away in flesh, for one greedy body to grow fat with food gained from another, for one live creature to go on living through the destruction of another living thing. . . . Make not their flesh your food, but seek a more harmless nourishment. . . . Take not away the life you cannot give. For all things have an equal right to live.

OVID, *Metamorphoses*, 10 A.D.

The Bad Genii have execrable feasts, made up into dishes. But the Superior Daemons are regaled with whole Gardens and Orchards of most delectable fruits and flowers silently sent forth by the Spirit of Nature.

SIR HENRY MORE,
Immortality of the Soul, 1680

Man is the butcher and the tomb of his brother animals.

ALEXANDER POPE, *Times of Innocence*, 1733

Man alone consumes and engulfs more flesh than all other animals put together. He is, then, the greatest destroyer, and he is so more by abuse than by necessity.

GEORGE LOUIS LECLERC DE BUFFON,
L'Histoire Naturelle, 1749

It is a cruel folly to offer up to ostentation so many lives of creatures, as make up the state of our treats.

WILLIAM PENN,
Fruits of Solitude, 1792

When there is plenty of vegetables, no meat is necessary.

A Lady, *The Cook's Complete Guide*, 1827

I have no doubt that it is a part of the destiny of the human race, in its gradual improvement, to leave off eating animals, as surely as the savage tribes have left off eating each other. . . . He will be regarded as a benefactor of his race who shall teach man to confine himself to a more innocent and wholesome diet.

HENRY DAVID THOREAU,
Walden, 1854

Our monstrous habit of bringing millions of animals into existence for the purpose of barbarously slaughtering them, roasting their corpses and eating them.

GEORGE BERNARD SHAW,
On Going to Church, 1896

4

To Kill or Not to Kill: Flesh Foods Versus Plants

*T*HIS book on simple food is vegetarian, of course. It is the simplest, cleanest, easiest way to eat. I take it for granted that to live on plants and fruits, seeds and nuts is the way for rational, kindly and perceptive people to live. By the time mankind has fully advanced from complex back to simple living, flesh will have been dropped from the diet and that cruel costly fare will be left to the carnivores. The readers of this book may be beyond that repulsive custom, but for those who are not, I set down what I consider legitimate arguments for a vegetable diet. However, I realize in advance I shall make little dent upon the general public, long-time confirmed in its savage custom.

The sight of slabs of flesh should horrify and disgust any sensitive person if they exercised their inborn compassion. Habit has dimmed their native kindliness. Their palates have become abnormally corrupted and conditioned by a taste for dead food, its flavoring and odors. People who eat slaughtered creatures every day find it hard to imagine what to substitute for meat, not realizing that meat is the substitute for vegetables.

> A Cook being bidden by his Master to dress him a peece of flesh; he asked of him Cheese and Oile to make the sawce; to whom his Master answered: away, fool, away; if I had either Cheese or Oile, what needed I to have bought a peece of flesh?
> THOMAS MOFFETT,
> *Helth's Improvement,* 1600

Nature has provided man with an abundance of food for full nourishment instead of putrefying corpses, which repugnant diet decent folk would abhor if generation upon generation had not, through use and custom, habituated themselves to the ghoulish practice of making their stomachs the burial ground for dead bodies.

> I wonder of what sort of feeling, mind, or reason, that man was possessed who was first to pollute his mouth with gore, and to allow his lips to touch the flesh of a murdered being; who spread his table with the mangled forms of dead bodies, and claimed as daily food and dainty dishes what but now were beings endowed with movement, with perception, and with voice?
> PLUTARCH,
> *On the Eating of Flesh,* 70 A.D.

> It is only by softening and disguising dead flesh by culinary preparation that it is rendered susceptible of mastication or digestion, and that the sight of its bloody juices and raw horror does not excite loathing and disgust.   PERCY BYSSHE SHELLEY,
> *A Vindication of Natural Diet,* 1813

However, I do agree with Gandhi that many a meat-eater who may be kindly and considerate is a better man than a strict vegetarian who beats his wife. We knew one self-righteous vegetarian (a fanatical new convert) who, entertaining us for dinner, ignominiously relegated his wife and daughter, still flesh-eaters, to the kitchen to eat while we were served with our host in the dining room. This hardhearted purist had much to learn about right living, although he was on the track to right diet.

The word "vegetarian" derives from the Latin "vegetus"—whole, sound, fresh, lively. The meat humans eat is neither whole, sound, fresh or lively. It is dis-limbed, tainted, decaying, stale and dead. A diet consisting of green leafy vegetables, root crops, grains, berries, nuts and fruits supplies all the body needs for strength and well-being. It is healthful food, aesthetic, economical, harmless to our brother animals, easy to grow, to prepare and to digest.

Flesh-eating by humans is unnecessary, irrational, anatomically unsound, unhealthy, unhygienic, uneconomic, unaesthetic, unkind and unethical. May I elaborate?

Unnecessary: Meat is not a necessity but a cultivated want. We need not butcher our fellow creatures for food. Millions of people throughout the world and through the ages have lived their whole lives on plant food and been none the worse; in fact, they have probably been in better health because of their abstemious diet. I had the good sense to be born in a vegetarian family and have lived into my seventies in good health and strength, without meat. Scott became a vegetarian in his mid-thirties and has lived into his nineties, hale and hearty, with plenty of brain and brawn, and without meat. It is obviously not necessary to eat cooked flesh.

A vegetarian friend, Henry Bailey Stevens, wrote some *Rhymes for Meat-Eaters,* from one of which I quote:

> With lentils, tomatoes and rice, olives and nuts and bread,
> Why does a man care to gnaw a slice of something
> bleeding and dead?

With honey, banana and pear, orange and corn and beet,
Why does he feel he must tear into some carcass meat?
How does his nose go astray, what in his instinct warps,
That he wants to ravish and slay, in order to feed on a corpse?

Irrational: The argument is frequently made that if
we did not kill and eat animals, the creatures would take
over and cover the earth. This is not necessarily so. The
process of natural selection would intervene as it does
with wild animals. If we stopped breeding and cozening
domestic animals, the rate of their population growth
would immediately and drastically diminish.

Animals need not be bred; they need not be killed;
they need not be eaten. "But it is natural for us to eat
animals" is the usual remark—"Animals were made for
us." That is hardly logical. Animals were on the earth
aeons before man. They waited long before their de-
vourers arrived.

If it were so natural, why not catch and kill your own
animal, cut a slice from the carcass or tear off a leg of the
living beast and eat it "naturally," fresh and whole? You
could do that with a fruit or a vegetable, but not with
your pet cat or dog's quivering flesh. Many who claim to
love animals and have them for pets would never kill and
eat their own Bunny Boy. But others' pets, other animals' offspring and parents that have been murdered by
others, can be put into the stew pot and callously consumed.

She, indignantly: "The cat has eaten our pet bird."
He, determinedly: "The wicked beast shall die."
Then he resumed his quail on toast, and she her pigeon pie.

Some animal lovers' interest in animals is often most
intense in the vicinity of the stockpot. An ancient folio,

The Shepherd's Calendar (1493) has the anonymous author speak fondly to the snail about to be cooked: "Never does Lombard eat thee in such sauce as *we* make for thee. We put thee in a big plate, with black pepper and onions."

> Carnivora, you call savage and ferocious—lions and tigers and serpents—while yourselves pollute your hands with blood and come behind them in no species of barbarity. And yet for them murder is the only means of sustenance; whereas to you it is a superfluous luxury. Why do you belie the Earth as though she were unable to feed and nourish you? You have a super-abundance of all the necessaries of existence. In point of fact, it is not the lions and wolves we kill to eat, as we might do in self-defense. On the contrary, we leave them unmolested; and yet the innocent and the domesticated and helpless—these we kill.
>
> PLUTARCH,
> *On the Eating of Flesh*, 70 A.D.

> Some people are not to be persuaded to taste of any creatures they have daily seen and been acquainted with while they were alive: others refuse what they fed and took care of themselves, yet all of them feed heartily and without remorse on beef, mutton and fowls when they are bought in the market.
>
> BERNARD DE MANDEVILLE,
> *Fable of the Bees*, 1723

Most meat-eaters have a squeamish limit beyond which even they will not go. They will not eat worms, slugs, garden snails (though they are said to be an excellent source of protein), or insects, mice, rats, cats or dogs, horses, or human beings. "The Samoans, who eat dogs, despise eggs and chickens. Similarly, the Qitoto of Brazil, who eat rats, frogs, lizards, snakes and turtles, eat the eggs of reptiles but despise those of birds."[1] Bernard Shaw spoke of meat-eating as "cannibalism with its he-

[1] Mark Graubard, *Man's Food, Its Rhyme or Reason*, 1943

41

roic dish omitted." And Bronson Alcott remarked to Emerson who was dilating upon the horrors of cannibalism while carving up a roast: "But, Mr. Emerson, if we are to eat meat at all, why should we not eat the best?" I would agree, in that I have often thought a baby's chubby arm looks delicious and (if I ate flesh) good enough to munch on.

Anatomically Unsound: Animals (and man is one of them) are structurally and functionally adapted to a particular mode of nutrition. The rabbit, to which a vegetarian is often disparagingly compared, is of the Rodentia order, feeding entirely on vegetable matter. The pig is an Omnivora; its diet is closest to the typical human omnivorous diet of today. The domesticated pig is not particular about what it eats. Like millions of contemporary humans, its diet includes practically anything edible, of both animal and vegetable origin.

Physiologically, a fruit and vegetable diet is more in line with the human anatomy. The teeth, the digestive system, the hands, feet and mammary glands of humans resemble the ape family to a great extent.

> Primitive humanity was, no doubt, like the anthropoids, mainly frugiverous. ROBERT BRIFFAULT,
> *The Mothers,* 1927

The digestive juices of man are not sufficient to tackle what the carnivores eat. The carnivores secrete hydrochloric acid about ten times as strong as that of humans and have a very short intestinal tract so that meat is quickly digested and expelled. Man's digestive tract is three times as long, holds food for two or three days, forming a putrefying mess if on a meat diet.

The structure of the teeth gives an important clue as

to the natural food of a species. Flesh-eating animals have tusks and fangs for tearing and gnawing; herbivores and frugivores have smooth teeth for grinding and chewing. Man and gorilla both belong to the frugivora family. Our front teeth are for biting and our back teeth for crushing and pulping; therefore human diet should be similar to that of the apes: raw fruit, raw vegetables, nuts, shoots and sprouts.

> Certainly Man by Nature was never made to be a Carnivorous Creature: nor is he arm'd at all for Prey and Rapin, with gag'd and pointed Teeth and crooked Claws, sharpened to rend and tear: but with gentle Hands to gather Fruit and Vegetables, and with Teeth to chew and eat them.　　　JOHN RAY,
> *Historia Plantarum,* 1686

Unhealthy: During World War II Denmark was put on emergency rations and the king called for a meatless program for a year. Denmark established a world record for lowered death rate that year and a marked decrease in the illness rate. Going back to meat-eating the next year sent the death rate back to the pre-war level.

The strongest of animals, the bull, the elephant, the gorilla, the hippopotamus, are all vegetarian. The camel, also a vegetarian, has long endurance records; the horse and deer have speed records.

> A farmer says to me, "You cannot live on vegetable food solely, for it furnishes nothing to make bones with"; and so he religiously devotes a part of his day to supplying his system with the raw materials of bones; walking all the while he talks behind his oxen, which, with vegetable-made bones, jerks him and his lumbering plough in spite of every obstacle.
> HENRY DAVID THOREAU,
> *Walden,* 1854

As to the vaunted necessity for protein and the high protein content in animal flesh and animal products to maintain robust health: protein is certainly required in the body for growth and repair, but is there not a maximum as well as a minimum beyond which one should not go? Too much protein overtaxes the vital organs. The excess must be eliminated as waste or be stored in the muscles, which become hard and inflexible. One might well ask: How little protein does one require, not how much does one need?

There is protein in nuts, beans, peas, lentils, mushrooms, cheese, milk, eggs, wholemeal cereals, and many green vegetables. Practically no common foodstuff is devoid of some protein. Plants manufacture it from the nitrogen of the air. They make the simpler type of protein, but the same amino acids as in meat.

Vegetable protein is the original source of meat protein. Nuts are not a substitute for meat; meat is a substitute for nuts. All fruits average out with about as much protein as in mother's milk. The banana has more protein than mother's milk. Vegetables average out to about 3 percent protein, nuts to 15 percent and seeds about 20 percent.

If one fed adequately on fresh vegetables, fruits, nuts, seeds and sprouts one could do without animal flesh and dairy products and still be above the minimum necessary intake recommended by orthodox nutritionists.

Unhygienic: It is not only healthier but cleaner to eat fresh vegetables and fruits instead of putrefying meat. Animal carcasses are often full of poisons and sicknesses, and of food additives and chemicals that have been used to fatten or soften or preserve the corruptible flesh. These poisons go into the human bodies that consume the dead meat. With a carnivorous diet the human is a

44

tomb for animal disease. Dead animal bodies contain heavy concentrations of toxic wastes, virulent bacteria and are often diseased with tumors, cancers, tuberculosis, swine fever, and other dangers to health.

> Most meats available today are virtually saturated with antibiotics, hormones, tranquilizers, pesticides, dyes, deodorants, and radiation. . . . The majority of processed meats contain preservatives, stabilizers, plastic residue, and other harmful substances.
> *The Mother Earth News,*
> No. 2, "Meat Is No Treat,"

No one knows better than meat inspectors how much disease there is among animals slaughtered for food. A woman attended a banquet and ordered a vegetable plate. At her side sat a stranger who also chose a vegetable plate. "You too are a vegetarian?" she asked him. "No, madam," he replied, "I am a meat inspector."

Uneconomic: Too many thousands of acres of valuable fertile land are being devoted to pasturage or fodder-feed for animals that are fattened to be eaten by man: over half of all agricultural land in the United States. This land could be planted with crops for direct, firsthand feeding to man, a much quicker and economical way of obtaining food than at secondhand, through animal's bodies. An estimated 40 percent of the world's livestock production is derived from vegetable sources that could be used for human food.

There is supposed to be about one acre per person in the world for food production. Meat-eaters take nearly two acres to feed the animals they eat. It is more ecologically and economically sound to devote fertile land to human food than to pass choice grains and legumes through the bodies of cattle. One acre of grazing land produces forty-three pounds of food protein when planted in soybeans, which are nutritionally equal to meat, are cheaper, containing less fat, and with less chance of communicable diseases.

> The amount of protein that can be produced on an acre of land by dry beans, peas or soybeans would meet the requirement of one person for 1,116, 1,785 and 2,224 days respectively. Beef, pork or poultry so produced would meet the requirements for 77, 129 and 185 days respectively. *Bio-Dynamic* magazine, No. 126

> For a given area of land, some ten times as many calories can be produced in the form of cereals or root crops than in the form of meat, eggs, milk, cheese. DR. JOHN YUDKIN,
> *Sweet and Dangerous,* 1972

Vegetarianism could go far toward solving the world food problem by eating lower on the food chain. To feed the world's population more adequately and economically, the enormous quantities of grains, pulses and legumes fed to farm stock animals should be drastically curtailed or eliminated entirely.

Unaesthetic: The revolting slabs and gobbets of flesh that are displayed and hung in butcher shops, or slickly plastic-packaged in supermarkets, would shock any fairly sensitive or artistic person who could bring himself to view the sight objectively. Aesthetically, fruits and vegetables are certainly more attractive than cut-up carcasses and ground-up pieces of flesh, raw and red, or roasted or broiled.

Walter de la Mare wrote a poem about a butcher shop.

> I can't abear a Butcher, I can't abide his meat,
> The ugliest shop of all is his, The ugliest in the street:
> Baker's are warm; cobbler's dark; chemists burn watery light;
> But oh, the sawdust butcher's shop, that ugliest of sights!

Ruskin has lyricized: "The criterion of a beautiful action or of a noble thought is to be found in song, and an action about which we cannot make a poem is not fit for humanity." Did he ever apply this test to flesh-eating?

> I rarely used animal food, not so much because of any ill effects which I had traced to them, as because they were not agreeable to my imagination. The repugnance to animal food is not the effect of experience, but is an instinct. I believe that every man who has ever been earnest to preserve his higher or poetic faculties in the best condition has been particularly inclined to abstain from animal food. — HENRY DAVID THOREAU, *Walden*, 1854

Unkind: Let's look at meat-eating from the animal's point of view. They have rights not to be infringed on. They love their lives and their families. Wild creatures are hunted and killed cruelly with no compassion. Domestically bred animals are wrenched from their families, transported callously and carelessly to abattoirs; there, frenzied with fear at the crowding, the mutual cries and the stench, they are pole-axed, hooked on moving belts for final slaughter, their throats cut, their dangling, twisting, agonized bodies slashed and skinned often before all of life is extinct. I know, because I've seen it on two horrifying visits to slaughterhouses in Chicago twenty-five years ago.

There is a sad song from the thirteenth century, found in the library of a Bavarian Benedictine monastery. Here is one verse of "Cignus usted Cantat":

> Once I dwelt in the lakes, Once I was a beautiful swan.
> O miserable me! Now I am roasted black!
> I am borne upon a platter and can no longer fly.

47

I catch sight of gnashing teeth,
O miserable me! Now I am roasted black!

We cannot eat flesh without unkindness and violence and cruelty. Fish are dragged from their natural element with ferociously sharp hooks; whales' gigantic bodies are tracked in the sea and mercilessly stabbed until death; seals are murdered with clubs and stripped half-living of their skins; crabs and lobsters are boiled alive.

> We throw our Crabs alive into scalding Water, and tye our Lobsters to the Spit to hear them squeek when they are roasted, our Eels and Gudgeons jumping to avoid the Danger of the Frying-pan leap into the Fire. WILLIAM KING,
> *The Art of Cookery,* 1709

What about "humane killing" you may ask. How can one be cruel humanely? Killing is killing. It has been estimated that man kills in one day more cattle than carnivorous animals kill in a hundred years. Let me quote words from lofty philosophers on the cruel and gruesome, and human, custom of slaying and eating our fellow creatures.

> *William Cowper:* Earth groans beneath the burthen of a war waged with defenseless innocence.
> *Romain Rolland:* Thousands of animals are uselessly butchered every day without a shadow of remorse.
> *Pythagoras:* What a monstrous crime it is that entrails should be entombed in entrails; that one ravening body should grow fat on others which it crams into it; that one living creature should live by the death of another living creature.
> *Plutarch:* Why kill and martyr so cruelly these gentle beings who harm no one, but who are so useful to you, who aid you in your labour, are your faithful companions, and furnish you with clothing to cover you and milk to feed you? What more do you require

of them? Does not the ground produce sufficient fruits for your food?

Leo Tolstoy: It is not even the suffering and death of the animals that is so horrible but the fact that man, without any need for so doing, crushes his lofty feeling and mercy for living creatures and does violence to himself that he may be cruel.

Unethical: "How could you select such an occupation?" asked a horrified onlooker to a worker in the stockyards of Chicago. "We're only doing your dirty work, sir," was the scornful and silencing reply. Whoever eats the meat without killing the animal himself is having his dirty work done for him.

I know not which strikes me most forcibly in the ethics of this question—the injustice, the cruelty or the nastiness of flesh-eating. The injustice is to the butchers, the cruelty is to the animals, the nastiness concerns the consumers. With regard to this last in particular, I greatly wonder that persons of refinement—aye, even of decency—do not feel insulted on being offered, as a matter of course, portions of corpses as food! Such comestibles might possibly be tolerated during sieges, or times of other privation of proper viands in exceptional circumstances, but in the midst of a civilized community able to command a profusion of sound and delicious foods, it ought to be deemed an affront to set dead flesh before a guest!   ANNA KINGSFORD,
Addresses on Vegetarianism, 1912

We are not only killers; we are slave drivers and exploiters; we are food robbers. We rob the bees, for honey; we rob the chickens, for eggs; we rob the cows, for milk. Cattle in their wild state suckle their calves for fifteen months. Domesticated cows are pushed beyond their normal breeding capacity, separated from their calves often at birth and are fooled into giving us milk instead of to their calves. As to wild poultry, most birds

49

lay four or five eggs a year. Factory-farming forces domestic birds to lay hundreds.

Milk is food for the infant of its species. Eggs are food for the embryo bird. Neither should be consumed by human adults.

> The Egyptians for a great while durst not eat Eggs, because they are imperfect or liquid Flesh; neither did they eat a long time any Milk, because it is but discoloured Blood.
>
> THOMAS MOFFETT,
> *Helth's Improvement,* 1600

> Every egg contains a chicken: that is, the entire material wherewith to make one; and requires nothing to produce a living animal but a little rise in temperature, either naturally or artificially applied.
> SIR HENRY THOMPSON,
> *Food and Feeding,* 1880

> The egg too has a mind, doing what our able chemists will never do, building the body of a hatchling, choosing among the proteins: These for the young wing-muscles, these for the great crystalline eyes, these for the flighty nerves and brain: choosing and forming: a limited but superhuman intelligence.
> ROBINSON JEFFERS,
> *De Rerum Virtute,* 1963

Fowl and cattle and other domesticated animals live a sheltered but an unnatural existence, wholly dependent upon our power of life and death. We who interfere in their lives and participate in any way in their deaths are ethically responsible.

Aware of the almost universal abuse of our animal brothers, Scott and I, as vegetarians, have lessened our dependence on animal products. We drink no milk, eat no eggs (except what may come in dishes served away from home), wear no animal skins or coats of leather, and try to get nonleather belts and shoes. We are not purists, nor entirely consistent in our avoidance of harm to animals. We both eat honey, stolen from the bees. Scott eats yogurt, although he is turning to tofu, a soybean product. Aware of the vegetarian's need for vitamin B-12, we both eat some cottage cheese. I have a predilection for Dutch cheeses, having lived long in Holland, and my mother being Dutch. I also have a well-known (to my friends) liking for ice cream: a remnant from my misguided youth. This addiction is indulged in occasionally, at birthdays and other celebrations, when I may fall from grace. I have used buttermilk in journey cakes, and cheese occasionally in a cooked vegetable dish.

We are looked down on with some scorn by purist friends for using any dairy products. If there is egg or milk in something while traveling, we'll eat it. If there's meat, we won't. Inconsistent? Certainly. Who isn't, about many things? Is there a thoroughly consistent person on earth?

All diets are relative to the consciences of the eater. One cannot be perfectly consistent in living, but a more or less harmless way of life is possible, and if not as pure as the purest one can at least try to be not as gross as the grossest. Scott and I have worked out a diet for ourselves that reduces our exploitation of animals to a minimum. It keeps us in good health and is open to improvement as we learn more and experiment further.

There are pure and not so pure recipes in this book: none requiring eggs, few milk or cheese. There are some suggesting the use of honey and maple syrup, which we prefer for sweetening rather than any form of sugar. Maple syrup, which we made so plentifully in Vermont and which we now have to buy, is not entirely free of exploitation, as it involves tapping and draining, to some slight extent, of the life blood of the noble maple trees.

51

Slavery of animals to man is one thing. Men also exploit themselves and become slaves to animals. Breeders, milkers, shepherds, graziers, farmers, slaughtermen, all involve labor devoted to being valets and nursemaids to animals. The time and care would better be centered on breeding and caring for better human beings.

We humans are privileged animals. *We* will not be cooked for a cow's dinner or infected with a disease so that a monkey can find out the cause of its illness; or taught to run round and round in a wheel to make a squirrel laugh; or caged and our throats slit to make us sing sweetly for our supper; or locked behind zoo bars as examples of curious human beings, or our breast-milk stolen to give to calves. Nor will *our* babies be sent to the slaughterhouse and sliced up for someone's dinner.

"Waiter! Bring back the pudding!" called Alice. She cut a slice and handed it to the Red Queen. "What impertinence!" said the Pudding. "I wonder how you'd like it, if I were to cut a slice out of *you,* you creature!" LEWIS CARROLL,
Through the Looking Glass, 1896

There is a fierce rhyme called "Tit for Tat," set to music by one of my favorite composers, Benjamin Britten. Whether the words are his or not I could not trace. I heard the song sung at an International Vegetarian Congress in The Hague.

Have you been catching a fish, Tom Noddy?
Have you snared a weeping hare?
Have you whistled "No Nunny" and gunned a poor bunny?
Or blinded a bird of the air?
Have you trod like a murderer through the green woods,
Through the dewy deep dingles and glooms,
While ev'ry small creature cries shrill to Dame Nature:

"He comes! Run! Run! He comes!"?
Wonder I very much do, Tom Noddy, if ever when
  you are aroam,
An ogre from Space will stoop a lean face, and lug *you* home.
Lug you home over his fence, Tom Noddy, of thornstocks
  nine yards high,
With your knees strung round his old iron gun and your
  head dangling by:
And hang *you* up stiff on a hook, Tom Noddy, from a
  stone-cold pantry shelf,
Whence your eyes will glare in an empty stare, till you
  are cooked yourself!

Food habits can be changed, though they are one of
the strongest habits of the human family. It has been said
that an immigrant will abandon the language of his fa-
therland before he abandons the eating pattern on
which he was brought up. However, food patterns do
change. We no longer eat our fellow men, though we still
kill masses of them, to what purpose? An African canni-
bal, on hearing of the huge numbers of people killed in
modern wars, exclaimed, "Why all those men? You can't
eat so many!"

Many young people today are modifying the mores
they were born into, while thousands in our own acquaintance alone are trying new ways of preparing
and processing food. Hundreds that we know are
turning to vegetarianism as a more wholesome way of
eating.

There are those, of course, who scorn the "roots and
berries school" and see it as a fad of those who "feed on
rabbit or caterpillar food." I am fairly sure that diehards
for today's conventional meat diet who may happen to
read the preceding pages will never be moved to abandon their feeding on "putrid Carcasses of Dead Ani-

mals," as John Evelyn, that believer in "the wholesomeness of the Herby Diet," surmised in his *Acetaria* (1699):

> I am sufficiently sensible how far, and to how little purpose I am gone on this Topic: Our raw Sallet deckt in its best Trim, is never like to invite Men who have once tasted Flesh to quit and abdicate a Custom which has now so long obtained. . . . This is not my Business, further than to show how possible it is by so many instances and Examples, to live on wholesome Vegetables, both long and happily.

I acknowledge that leaving off meat-eating means taking the lives of plants when we cut off their lives, swallow and digest them. And I apologize to the radish, the carrot, the head of lettuce, the apple, the orange, when eating them. Some day, I hope, we shall be able to live on sunlight absorbed through the skin and deep breaths of clean air—though that also is teeming with minuscule forms of life.

So far, eat we must, in order to survive. Therefore we should look to the less sentient forms of life for sustenance. Life is inherent in every food substance that we imbibe, and one has to kill to eat, whether it be an apple, a tomato, or a blade of grass. By what right do we consume these marvels of nature? Plants have an important place on earth. I salute the trees and apologize if I cut one down. I shrink from picking a daisy or a pansy, or biting into an apple or radish. Who am I to take their lives in their prime?

We should widen the range of human feeling until it encompasses all life on earth, doing the most good to the greatest number and the least harm to the least number. Standards and relative degrees of harm and harmlessness will vary with each one of us. Some will continue to eat fish and fowl while eschewing red meat; some will eat nothing that walks or wiggles—still eating dairy products; some will eat no products at all of the animal kingdom—no eggs, milk, cheese or honey. But we can all be constantly aware of the rights of others, be it baby lamb, bison, fly or cauliflower. We can modify our food habits so that we approach the ideal of living on fruits and nuts and seeds which have finished their life cycle and with which the tree or bush or plant is finished.

The time will come in the world's history, and a movement is setting in that direction even now, when it will be deemed as strange a thing to find a man or a woman who eats flesh as food, as it is now to find a man or a woman who refrains from eating it. RALPH WALDO TRINE,
Every Living Creature, 1899

The time will come when men will look on the murder of animals as we now look on the murder of men. LEONARDO DA VINCI

*L*ET her dyet proceede more from the provision of her owne yarde, than the furniture of the markets; and let it be rather esteemed for the familiar acquaintance shee hath with it, than for the strangenesse and raritie it bringeth from other Countries. GERVASE MARKHAM,
The English Hus-wife, 1615

These Summer Fruits, when they have been gathered long, and exposed to the corrupt Air of Cities and Towns, the pure spiritous Vertues and digestive Faculty is in a manner destroyed. Green Food does often lie a considerable time before they are eaten. Especially in great Cities or Towns some of them lie heating together, as Beans and Pease, by which means they lose their pure brisk lively taste and smell. THOMAS TRYON,
The Way to Health, Long Life & Happiness, 1683

Some are of that mind that they value nothing but what is far fetcht, dear bought or hard to be had . . . Such is the vanity of this wicked world.
HANNAH WOOLLEY,
The Queenlike Closet, 1684

We have taken the Pains to find out such a multitude of different Foods which were unknown to our Ancestors that we have introduced a Cloud of Diseases which they knew nothing of. DR. M.L. LEMERY,
A Treatise of All Sorts of Foods, 1745

Preserve a good constitution of body and mind. To this a spare diet contributes much. Have wholesome, but no costly food. WILLIAM PENN,
Fruits of Solitude, 1792

Everyone who is so happy as to live in the country, and can gather vegetables daily from his own garden, knows the difference between them when gathered thus and properly cooked, and those which have been picked and kept for market even one night. SOLON ROBINSON,
Facts for Farmers, 1866

When the materials and cooking are of the best, the plainest, cheapest food has attractions which is seldom to be found in the most laboured attempts.
HENRY SOUTHGATE,
Things a Lady Would Like to Know, 1874

56

5

Complicate or Simplify:
Processed Versus
Fresh Foods

*U*NLESS we are incarcerated in a prison or in a hospital, where we are forced to take what we get, we can choose our nourishment. We can eat simple fresh food or we can eat store-bought fabrications. Nearly every food on the market nowadays is adulterated in one way or another with worthless or objectionable matter, or robbed of some of its vital elements. These fake, unnatural foods—conditioned, pasteurized, smoked, salted, sugared, colored and glossed-up—have little of nature left in them. They are not good-natured foods, but ill-natured.

There are three kinds of foodstuffs: those raw, vital and fresh, as found in nature; those cooked, with the vitality largely killed by high temperatures; and those manufactured, processed, deadened or poisoned. A guide to safer eating in a poisoned world might well be: avoid those foods that are imperishable. "Eat only those foods that spoil, or rot, or decay, but eat them before they do."[1]

[1]Dr. E.V. McCollum, Johns Hopkins University

Avoid all dead, denatured foods, such as white bread, white crackers, white sugar, polished rice, processed cheeses. "The four horsemen destroying our civilization are refined sugar, refined flour, hydrogenated oil, and gasoline fumes."[2] (I would add cigarette smoke and alcohol.)

When you are faced with food that has been sterilized, fumigated, hydrogenated, hydrolyzed, homogenized, colored, bleached, puffed, exploded, defatted, degermed, texturized, or if you don't know what has been done to it, the safest rule is not to eat it.

My friend, Woody Kahler, writes of how pickling and fixing food pays off. "It pays the research laboratories. It pays the drug-hucksters. It pays the doctors. It pays the hospitals. It pays the psychiatrists as long as your money lasts. It pays the funeral parlors."[3] He has also said: "Store food makes store teeth necessary."

With advancing civilization, our diet—along with much else in life—has undergone a thoroughgoing change. Big business has not yet monopolized air, sunshine, sleep, rest, or pure running water, but it has gained a monopoly on a large part of the food eaten in the world. This is a supermarket country, with the shelves of the stores filled with commodities packaged and preserved to keep until some customer, in his own good time, takes them off the shelf.

The preparation of food has become a form of mass production where it was once an individual craft. Hundreds of homesteaders we know are raising their food and saying, "Don't buy it; grow it. Use what you have instead of buying what you don't need." But the ads

[2]Dr. Carl C. Wahl, *Essential Health Knowledge*, 1966
[3]Woodland Kahler, *The Cravings of Desire*, 1960

blare out: Buy our easy foods. Here it is: all cleaned and cut up, sanitized, colored, flavored, fortified, dehydrated, treated to last: "breakfast foods, milled, grilled, baked-up, dried-up, puffed-up, roughed-up, packed in cardboard, kept for months, and sold at the pistol point of publicity campaigns."[4]

Convenience foods are flooding the market as outlets start up in shopping centers like mushrooms overnight. If a product can be made that will attract people, if customers will buy, consume, and come back for more; if that product can be made for a dime and sold for a dollar, then business reaps huge profits and cares little for the health of the consumer. Big profits may well spell bad nutrition for the population.

Chemicals and processing and packaging are what industry adds to good fresh food, not health. Lifeless materials, processed to a high degree of artificial perfection, are their stock in trade. Supermarkets and stores are interested in a rapid turnover of foods. Tickle the palate and eye of the customer, whether the customers' bodies are demoralized or not. A horrible example is a concoction of blueberry waffles, made with "sugar, cottonseed oil, salt, sodium carboxymethycellulose, silicon dioxide, citric acid, modified soy protein, artificial flavor and coloring, maltol, and blueberry solids," or so the package reads.

The U.S. food industry in 1969 used more than 90 million pounds of flavor and flavor-enhancing additives. In addition it used close to 800 million pounds of additives to improve the color, texture and keeping qualities of food. . . . From 2,500 to 3,000 food additives are now used in U.S. foods, including several leavening agents, 9 emulsifiers, 30 stabilizers and thickeners, 85 surfact-

[4]J. Wentworth Day, *Farming Adventure,* 1937

ants, 7 anti-caking agents, 28 anti-oxidants, 44 suquestrants, perhaps a dozen coloring materials, at least 8 acidulants, more than 30 chemical preservatives and over 1,100 flavoring ingredients. New additives are introduced each year. . . . America's bread industry used over 16 million pounds of chemicals a year, mostly leaveners, preservatives and anti-salin compounds. . . . In the summer of 1969 a British scientist patented a new additive that would make bread taste like bread. JAMES TRAGER, *Foodbook*, 1970

The human exposure to an increasing range of chemical additions in food is becoming frightful. Why should we continue to consume the synthetic materials that are currently being used in food products? "You may have to live in a crowd, but you do not have to live like it, nor subsist on its food."[5] Mark Hegstead, of Harvard's School of Public Health, is on the mild side when he says: "Thirty percent of the products of the grocery stores today could be thrown out and nobody be the worse." In fact, everybody would be much better off.

Junk foods cannot be made into good foods. I came across a cartoon depicting a group of little green men disembarking from their spaceship in Central Park in New York City. The leader says: "Remember, this is planet Earth. Here we don't breathe the air, drink the water, or eat the junk foods."

Let me pass on to readers some strong language from Mimi Sheraton, a noted writer and regular columnist on food for *The New York Times*. In an article in *Diversion* magazine (February, 1974), she castigated fabricated foods in round terms:

[5]Henry Van Dyke, *The School of Life*, 1925

The ever-increasing amount of junk food-in-sheep's clothing that is sold in supermarkets and restaurants is becoming everyday family fare. I walk up and down the aisles of any supermarket and see how firm a hold these gastronomic travesties have on the American palate. . . . Whether they are paper-wrapped, boxed, tubed, canned, frozen or dehydrated, they have been treated with artificial colorings and flavorings and enough preservatives to render them inertly non-perishable. . . . The freezer case contains almost nothing but junk foods. TV dinners offer soggy meats steamed under starchy gravies, vegetables as tasteless (and about as nutritious) as wet rags; potatoes that have been convenienced twice since they were made of powder dissolved in water, and pies that are like those Mother never made, even if Mother was the world's worst baker. . . . Cakes too damp, too sweet, and as artificial as paper roses. . . . Greasy canned gravies smelling like dog food and gloppy bottled salad dressing with their garlic and onion salts tasting like silver polish. . . . Pop-up-toaster-tarts that taste like no-name jam sandwiched between sheets of manila cardboard sealed with envelope glue. . . . Paper-thin hamburgers, limp gray, about as appetizing as wet scabs.

Some of these "gastronomic felonies" she likens to "instant swill." Could words be stronger and more apt? "What worries me," she continues, "are the thousands and millions of people, adults as well as children, who think these junk foods are really what food is supposed to be."

Here are equally violent slurs on current foods from *Esquire* magazine (June 1974) where Roy Andries de Groot writes about a commercial French dressing and a steak sauce:

The whole bloody business is completely overloaded with monosodium glutamate and sugar, but it also has an atmosphere of staleness, of eggs so old as to border on putrefaction, or rosemary that is as dry as hay, of ground nutmeg that has been on the shelf for five years, and of tarragon that has turned black with age. The slight sliminess on the tongue reeks of chemical preservatives. The smell is old rats in a haunted house. . . . The perfectly horrible contents [of the sauce] is a dreadful experience. There is a strong, overall atmosphere of mold and rottenness. A sense of deep putrefaction. It tastes the way the laundry basket smells after sweaty shirts have been in it for three days.

Nothing which I or my favorites of old have written could be more pungent or denunciatory than what these contemporary taste experts have to say, except perhaps this, from a 1709 book. After describing a profuse recipe with countless rich ingredients, the author "was easily persuaded from the Whimsicalness of the Composition and Garniture, that the properest vessel for a Physition to prescribe to send to the Table upon that occasion might be a Bed Pan."[6]

My advice would be: don't join the Americans who eat what is the palate-tickler of the moment nor fall for what may be highly touted on TV or radio or presented in the shrieking yowls of big-print bargains in the newspapers. The people who eat the junk foods are the deviants and faddists, not the "health food addicts," as we are called. The real food faddists go for the slot-machine meals, the factory foods, the cardboard pizzas, the sawdusty cereals whose packages cost more than their contents, the soda of ill-fame and the spongy sodium-propionated breads.

The present American plenteous but unhealthy diet of questionable counterfeit "convenience foods" is a problem that most of our countrymen face every day. In your trips to the supermarket you can avoid the processed potatoes, doughnuts, instant puddings, salad dressings, salted foods, carbonated beverages, preserves, pickles, fried snacks, condiments, puffy white-floured breads, white sugar and candies.

[6]William King, *The Art of Cookery,* 1709

It should be elementary knowledge nowadays to choose natural unrefined simple foods which have not been deprived of their essential food elements through manufacturing and preserving. But most of the population of the United States today, and of the civilized world, have been habituated, perverted, and poisoned with unnatural foods.

Consider the strange eating habits of civilized man who eats in restaurants, airplanes or bars, in artificially lighted and curtained enclosures full of bad air and canned noise. He dines upon cold-storage long-dead carcasses, canned and embalmed foods that may have been on shelves for years and on the stove for hours, and pours concocted sauces over this decaying food to titillate jaded palates. An affluent diet indeed!

Let us leave the mercantile and complex economy to stew in its own acrid juice while we seek out a simpler, wholesome, easy way to feed ourselves. It is for us to choose whether we eat "store stale" or "garden fresh" food.

> What I love most is an abundance of simple food of perfect quality and staggering freshness, very simply and respectfully treated, tasting strongly of itself.   SYBILLE BEDFORD,
> in *The Artist's & Writer's Cook Book,* 1961

I want to reduce food, and cooking, to the lowest possible denominator, to make the simplest, cheapest meals —the most easily prepared and served. If I know a simple way to make up a salad or prepare a vegetable, I'll tell it to you. If you can work out a simpler way, fine, go to it, and let me know how. If a more complicated mixture appeals to you, go to it, but don't let me know. It would be wasted on me; I'd never try it. For me, food at its best is the closest to nature and the most natural, though I would hardly go as far as the old person of Leeds, for simple indeed were his needs. Said he, "To save toil, growing things in the soil—I'll just eat the packet of seeds." That may perhaps be carrying simplicity too far.

Scott and I were in Japan some years ago and wandered about the countryside quite on our own, with only a Japanese phrase book to help us in tight corners. In a small local restaurant beside Lake Hakone, in view of Mount Fujiyama, with the aid of our phrase book we pointed at the meat dishes, shook our heads and hands, and said, "No, No! We want a meal *without* meat," and pointed at the word "without." The waiter, whose English was as minimal as was our Japanese, bowed and went into the kitchen to fill the order. After quite a long wait, and a discussion heard through the swinging doors, out came the proprietor or chef, who said to us in broken English, "We would like to serve you your desires, but, please, what kind of meat is 'without meat'?"

This book of mine is a very "without" book: without meat, of course, or fish or fowl; without white sugar and white flour, baking soda and powder; without pepper and salt (unless you use sea salt), without eggs and milk; without breads and pies and pastries. What is left, you will ask, for most people? Prisoner fare, hardship, you will say.

This good woman fed, and wished to feed others, like the beasts of the field, who are contented with grass today and grass tomorrow, so long as their hunger is allayed, without regard to the gratification of higher tastes.

A Lady, *The Lady's Companion*, 1851

What is left? We have all the fruits, all the vegetables and all the whole grains to eat. There are so many good things it is hard for me to make a selection. I could double the recipes I can find room for in this book. I can assure you that we do not starve at home. We are well fed and even often overfed.

The objection may still be made that most people cannot live upon the same simple things for seven days in the week and twelve months in the year. But many of our sturdy forefathers on this continent lived just that way. The author of *Pioneers of Old Ontario* tells of the diet of "the farthest north white man" for whom "it was often potatoes and cabbage for meals one day, varied by cabbage and potatoes the next."[7] Luckily, says another writer, "In times of stress the average frontier housewife had a facility, amounting almost to genius, for preparing tasty and satisfying meals from the most meager resources."[8]

The diet can vary with the seasons: In winter, solider and heavier food, more root crops, dried beans, potatoes, turnips. In spring and summer, lighter foods —asparagus, dandelion, green peas, tomatoes, cucumbers. Use the productions of the different seasons and of different climates, and catch them at their peak and in their youth. There is a Scottish proverb: "He that eats but ae dish seldom needs the doctor." Eating one food at a time, and while it is in season, is a good rule to follow.

Scott has told me a story of his friend, the Reverend John Holmes, a notable New York and Boston clergyman, who was being interviewed by a reporter for the *Daily Worker* while he was eating his breakfast in a stylish hotel dining room. Holmes was served strawberries and cream in February. Embarrassed at being

[7]W. L. Smith, *Pioneers of Old Ontario*, 1923
[8]Edward Everett Dale, *The Food of the Frontier*, 1947

caught eating such rich out-of-season food before a member of the proletariat, Holmes offered some to his interlocutor. "No, thanks," was the rather grim reply. "It might spoil my taste for prunes."

Mentioning the *Daily Worker* and the proletariat prods me to remark that I may seem to have written this book as though plenty of food were available to all, and we only had to pick out the most nourishing. I well know there are millions of people in the world today who are starving or on the brink of starvation, and who would grab any item to stuff down their empty gullets. Who can gainsay for them "the undue significance a starving man attaches to food," as Emily Dickinson so sardonically points out in one of her poems.

Simple eating need not be monotonous. Every meal of every day can vary if you like, but don't be afraid of sameness. If you find a good thing that you like, stick to it. Variety is not necessarily the spice of life, or of cooking. Appetite is. If you have excessive variety you eat too much. You flit from one thing to another and go back to the first, starting all over again and eating more than you need. All goes slopping down in quick-time, with little chewing. In cooking as in eating, give your attention to fewer items and learn to appreciate them.

> Simplify, simplify. Instead of three meals a day, if it be necessary, eat but one; instead of a hundred dishes, five; and reduce other things in proportion. HENRY DAVID THOREAU, *Walden,* 1854

Food can be not only simple in its choice and preparation and its serving, it can be simply produced, at home, in your own garden. If you eat only plants and fruits, a small acreage can grow the food you need at little extra expense or trouble. Cover your allotted garden space with a heavy mulch, in the fall, of hay or seaweed or autumn leaves, or, if you are not averse to such by-products, animal manure. Let the mulch lie on the ground all winter. In the early spring, cover it with compost and dig it in. Plant seeds and tend your crops as the sun's rays and the weather mature the plants. Use no sprays, dusts or chemical poisons. Pick from the garden in summer what you need for the day's food. Eat it fresh and whole and largely unprocessed. It can be out of the garden and on the table or over the fire in ten minutes.

> The humblest of self-grown, whole-eaten foods are both more palatable and more life-giving than the richest and most exotic —the most meretriciously dressed up and deceitfully doctored.
>
> H.J. MASSINGHAM,
> *This Plot of Earth*, 1944

The objects of cookery have been aptly outlined in an 1824 book: "1. To dress victuals so as to increase their healthfulness and preserve their nutritious qualities; 2. To do this in the most economical way—without waste; 3. To do this in the way most savoury to the palate, consistent with health."[9] I would add: 4. to reduce the fuss of food and eating to a minimum; 5. to work out a pattern of living on a homestead basis, so that food can be grown on the place, eliminating transportation, middleman profits and excessive production costs, and getting it fresh, on the spot.

Simple food (fruits, nuts, vegetables), simply grown (organically), simply prepared (with little peeling or cutting up), simply cooked (lightly braised, blanched,

[9]Thomas Cooper, *A Practical System of Domestic Cookery*, 1824

steamed or baked), simply garnished (with chopped-up tender greens and no sauces or gravies), simply served (from stove to table in saucepan, with one wooden bowl for each person for the whole meal), or, better still, eaten raw: What could be simpler, unless you eat standing, and pick from the trees?

> Here, here I live with what my board can with the
>   smallest cost afford,
> Though ne'er so mean the viands be, they will content
>   my Prue and me.
> On pea, or bean, or wort, or beet, whatever comes,
>   content makes sweet:
> We eat our own, and batten more, because we feed
>   on no man's score.

ROBERT HERRICK,
Epigram Complete, 1670

Part Two

PREPARING THE GOOD FOOD

Which dish in this poore Feast of Receipts is for your taste, Gentle Reader, I knowe not, for they are as various as men's pallates; yet must I hazard amongst the multitude, and though the subject I write of hath been handled by many, and many of a great deale more merit, yet I have runne so farre from the lisping affectation of ill imbrodred speech, or from the rude plainnesse of too much dulnesse, that when my booke shall be paraleled with others, it will speake sufficiently to get it selfe a free passage, nothing being in it I hope unworthy, nothing that may not very well authorize imitation. Neither do I ascribe to my selfe the grounds of every invention, for there be many due to such excellencies as others provided and I do thank them well.

GERVASE MARKHAM,
Hobson's Horse-Load of Letters, 1613

*I*F you know better precepts than these, candidly tell me; if not, follow them, as I do.   QUINTUS HORATIUS FLACCUS,
Satires, 35 B.C.

If perchaunce any list to picke a quarrell with my Receipts, as not being either proper or not ful, if I may obteine of him to beare with me til he himselfe shall have set foorth a better, or til the next impression, and the meanewhile (consydering that it is easier to reprehend a man's doings than to amend it) use me as a whet stone to further himselfe.   D. REMBERT DODOENS,
A Nievve Herball, 1578

And though amongst these mine owne conceits there happen a few to faile: yet seeing they are such as carry both good sense and probabilitie with them, I hope in your courtesies I shall find you willing to excuse so small a number, because I doubt not but that you shall finde good satisfaction in the rest.
SIR HUGH PLATT, *Floraes Paradise,* 1608

These experiments which I once thought should have slept in the grave with me are true and easie, a plain form of doing things by a nearer and safer way than ever hath hitherto been discovered.   GERVASE MARKHAM,
Countrey Contentments, 1613

I do not pretend to teach the old experienced Housekeeper, or those whose Knowledge is superior to mine; but should any thing be found in the following Sheets of Service to them, it would give me great Pleasure. Some Rules for the Young and Inexperienced I flatter myself will not be looked on as impertinent.   HANNAH GLASSE,
The Servant's Directory, 1760

The receipts for each article are formed on so easy and cheap a Plan, as to be within the Purchase of all ranks of People.
WILLIAM AUGUSTUS HENDERSON,
The Housekeeper's Instructor, 1800

Study the entire book with attention, for it is a record of things most necessary to success in housekeeping, which young housewives generally attain through many trying experiences.   JULIET CORSON,
Family Living on $500 a Year, 1888

70

6

On Recipes in General

SOME of the recipes in this collection are pure inspiration, right off the top of my head; some are *force
majeur*, as necessity dictated—all there was to work
with; some are adaptations of others' bright ideas, and
some are just good old stand-bys—what your own grandmother or great-grandmother made simply and well.

For elementary basic foods I cannot imagine that a
recipe is necessary, even for the rankest beginner. One
forever-to-be-nameless writer I came across took the
trouble to explain in detail how to make a so-called "do-
it-yourself" peanut butter sandwich: "Spread two tablespoons of peanut butter on one slice of bread," she wrote
out meticulously. "Top with a second slice of bread. Cut
in half. Place on plate and serve."

My recipes are simple but not that simpleminded.
Who has to be told how to bake a potato? Just scrub it
clean and put it into the oven and bake till forkable. Or
how to cook corn? Strip the husks, drop into boiling
water and take out in a couple of minutes. Or how to

make applesauce? Halve and core a sufficient number of apples, cut into pieces, simmer in a little water till tender, adding sweetening, if any, just before serving.

This is meant to be a book of general cooking directions on how to keep things simple. Therefore the recipes, and the directions, will tend to be simple. Proportions and exact amounts are not always given. In some of the simpler, one need not be specific. I give a rough outline that you can fit in with your own design.

If my editor would allow, my recipes would literally say "a handful of this; a bit of that." Not "two small onions," but "some onions." Add lemon juice if you have it. When herbs are called for, use what is at hand. Leave yourself some leeway. Take as many potatoes as you think you will want. When parsley is plenty, use aplenty; when it is scarce you can do with less. Sweeten as you go along. Use a little or a lot.

Where the proportions are left vague it is because there is actually a very wide range within which a good dish can be made. Experiment. Play games. Try a few unlikely additions to a favorite recipe. You need never make it again if you don't like it.

Or, if you are less adventurous, make a reputation for one or another good thing that you can make well. If you get expert in it no one will realize how limited your range really is. Apparently my forte is vegetable soup. On the strength of that, many people think I am a good cook. But I don't know how to tell you how to make my soups. I merely cut up any number and amount of any vegetables in almost any order (though the tougher should go into the pot first), braise some onions, add a little of this and that, and cook it.

Recipes, to my mind, should be purposely left vague, so that one can branch out and use what one has. Fairly indefinite directions have come down to us in ancient cookbooks. "Butter the size of a walnut" was probably one of the first attempts at exact measurements. Here are excerpts from recipes taken from two fifteenth-century manuscripts in the British Museum. "Take kowe mylke a good quantite . . . Put Sugre y-now into the potte . . . Use ote-mele a grate hepe . . . Make the dish poynaunt with spycery . . . Boil for a good while and serve it all abroad in dishes."

One of the most characteristic features of the old receipts is their vagueness. . . . As a rule, in the old books no definite quantity of meat or fish or of anything else is specified, and the proportions are left to the judgment of the cook. As an inevitable result, a cook of experience easily became indispensable and ran no risk of dangerous competition.   WILLIAM EDWARD MEAD,
The English Medieval Feast, 1931

You shall take as many carrots as you will and scrape them well and cut them in pieces, and cook them.   A Citizen of Paris,
Le Menagier de Paris, 1393

Let it seethe till it is done . . . For Ryce, let it boyle till it be something bigge . . . And when the Onions be through boyled take them off.   THOMAS DAWSON,
The Good Huswife's Jewell, 1587

Put into it a pound of butter or more, according to your quantity.   WILLIAM PENN, JR.,
My Mother's Receipts for Cookerys, 1702

Here is a typical sketchy recipe from an old Scotch cookbook: "Take a peerie [little] grain o' flo'or; a peerie grain o' mayle [oatmeal], a peerie grain o' butter, a peerie grain o' shuggar; a peerie grain o' trekkle." Or this, from an Irish cook: "You must take more than you'd think of flour, ma'am, just what you know of butter, the slightest taste in life of baking powder, and the fill of the small jug of milk."

Here is a conversation about a cryptic recipe: "But if we had eggs," Elizabeth asked, "how many would it take?" "That depends. If you have a dozen eggs, you use a dozen eggs. If you have three or four, you use three or four." "Well, how much flour would it take?" "That would depend on how many eggs." These cooks seem reluctant to pass on their recipes.

> How personal good cooking was, may be illustrated by an actual instance which occurred in Virginia back in the 1850s. A young lady went to the family cook and said, "Aunt Chloe, I wish you would tell me how to make that cake we had for supper." The answer was, "Well, Miss Agnes, I don't know as I can tell you. Well, take half a dozen eggs, if you got them, and then—you just go ahead as you knows and makes it."
>
> WILLIAM CHAUNCY LANGDON,
> *Everyday Things in American Life*, 1941

Perhaps the most ambiguous of all is a recipe for gingerbread I found in an *Old Farmer's Almanac:* "I always take some Flour; just enough for the Cakes I want to make: I mix it up with some Buttermilk if I happen to have it, just enough for the Flour; then I take some Ginger: some like more, some like less. I put in a little Salt and Pearlash, and then I tell John to pour in Molasses till I tell him to stop."

Here's another gingerbread recipe (from the fifteenth century) that doesn't even mention ginger!

> Take a quart of honey and seethe it and skim it clean. Take saffron, powdered pepper, and throw thereon. Take grated bread and make it so stiff that it will be leched. Then take cinnamon powder and strew thereon enough. Then make it square as

though thou wouldst slice it. Take, when thou slicest it, and cast box leavens above, stuck thereon in cloves. And if thou will have it red, colour it with saunders enough.

One more recipe from an old cookbook I must share with you: "The rule for sweetening gooseberries, rhubarb and cranberries: put in what you think is right, and then turn around and put in as much more."

If the ingredients are simple and few, so can the instructions be simple and few. I came across these directions for cooking oatmeal: "Add enough meal to the boiling water until it becomes sufficiently thick to say 'pouff' when it cooks." The simplest recipe of all might be: cook till done.

Even some of our modern writers on food are as vague as the ancients: witness these ambiguous directives from Max Eastman, a friend of Scott's in their early years: "You take a certain amount of water—it doesn't matter how much, for you can add more or boil the mixture longer. Add a pinch of salt. The size of a 'pinch' has never been accurately determined and cannot be reasoned out. It must be left to the Unconscious."[1] (I warrant that was the first time the unconscious had been mentioned in a cookbook.)

> The terms "stiff," "thin," "hard," "soft" are very flexible and depend on the cook's point of view.　KATE DOUGLAS WIGGIN, *A Book of Dorcas Dishes & Family Recipes*, 1911

> "Roughly," he asked his uncle, "how long does it take to cook?" "Oh, I don't know. The time to go to the grocer's and back."
> X. MARCEL BOULESTIN, *A Londres Naguère*, 1930

[1] In *The Artist's & Writer's Cook Book*, ed. by Beryl Barr and Barbara Turner Sachs, 1961

"How many tablespoons shall I put in?" "Glory to Gideon," my mother would say. "Put in what you think is right. Put in as much as you need. Put in enough. That's all!"

ROBERT TRISTRAM COFFIN,
Mainstays of Maine, 1944

The recipe is for the record, and in practice is modified as the inspiration of the moment and the materials demand. . . . The best professionals seldom follow even their own recipes with much accuracy.   FLETCHER PRATT & ROBESON BAILEY,
A Man and His Meals, 1947

When the proportions are left vague it is because there is actually a very wide range within which a good dish can be made. . . . When the beginner has found his feet, then he will be wise to experiment.   WILSON MIDGELEY,
Cookery for Men Only, 1948

Every venture in cooking is really a new beginning, depending on how many or how much of this or that you have. Are the apples or onions large, or small? Have you olive oil to cook with, or only water? Is your fire hot, or only warm? Does your family tolerate garlic; can you slip some by? Is there any flour in the house? What can you use instead? How can you extemporize? When have you thrown in enough? A good cook should know when to stop.

This book doth not contain any composition or mixture which is not very easie to bee prepared, farre more pleasing to the palate, and not all chargeable to the purse, since you are at liberty to imploy as much or as little in the making and imbellishments of these Cakes and Junkets as your means, the times and your own occasions will permit you to bestow thereon.

M. MARNETTE,
The Perfect Cook, 1656

If you cannot come by all these things named, then you may place some other thing at your discretion in the place.

JOHN MURRELL,
Two Books of Cookerie, 1631

As to quantities in my recipes: most will be for three or four people of good appetite. If you have a hungry horde to feed, these recipes can be doubled. But if picky people are present, then the food will go for five or six. What kind of eaters will they be? Are they outdoor workers, or bank employees, sitting all day, or TV watchers? Will they come in from skiing and skating, or from a tea party? Are they healthy, ravenous, or sated and disdainful? Are they fat and pallid and padded, or strenuous and slim? How good will your food be? Were you in a cooking mood or not? What else will be served? How many people will drop in unannounced? You may have to feed two or twenty. How do you know till they turn up? I never do, so I make up plenty.

My editor and I have a close and pleasant relationship on all but a few arrangements in this book. On details of recipe-writing our usually even tempers have been strained a bit. She wanted more than my telegraphic style and more detail. I resisted—especially on the number of people that each recipe would serve. We finally agreed that unless otherwise noted, each recipe would be for three or four normally hungry people.

Again, as to time of preparation: how can one say for someone else? Some cooks are diddlers and slowpokes. Some are efficient speed demons. Some are systematic workers, and some are sloppy and disorganized. Some will use slow wood stoves, and some will cook on quick radiant electric or gas stoves. All cooking times depend on the heat of the fire, and, when cooking with wood, every stick varies. Boiling and baking have to be approximate, depending on the wood used. There are more things to weigh than measurements and time periods in writing up a recipe.

I have said nothing about fires and stoves for cooking. I learned on an old wood cookstove and have never ventured cooking on gas or electricity. They may have their advantages in speed, but something is lost without the low steady heat a wood fire can supply.

> Slowness in cooking is one of the secrets of good cooking, gone from the world now where quick stoves and thin pots and pans rob us all of our birthright of flavor and tenderness. Many of my mother's best dishes (besides baked beans) depended upon hours and hours of slow cooking. The back of the stove, the cool half of the oven, were often more important than the hot and lower halves. Half of the flavor has gone out of the modern dishes because they are cooked fast, and with heat at one point only. Cooked? Electrocuted is the right word. Good cooking is slow cooking. Hours of serene development, as a rosebud forms and unfolds. So best kettles are the thick old iron ones, that hold and distribute heat in the round. The best frying-pans are thick as your hand. ROBERT TRISTRAM COFFIN,
> *Mainstays of Maine*, 1944

Anyone can learn in a minute or two which button to turn in a modern stove to get gradations of heat. It took more than a twist of the wrist to learn the temperatures of fires for dishes in olden times: "which should have a slow fire and yet a good one; which would lye long at the fire; which would have a quick and sharp fire without scorching; which should be suddenly and quickly dispatcht."[2]

[2]Gervase Markham, *The English Hus-wife*, 1615

An oven for bread-baking should be as hot as you could bear your hand in for twenty seconds, or whilst counting twenty. What is termed a quick oven is one in which you could hold your hand no longer than to count twenty-five. In a slow oven you could hold your hand to count thirty. MRS. T.J. CROWAN, *Every Lady's Cook Book*, 1854

Although I have never cooked according to a precise oven temperature, I realize many others are used to following heat in degrees. To my best estimate, the equivalent temperatures of my recipe instructions are as follows:

> slow oven—200°–250°
> warm oven—250°–300°
> moderate oven—350°
> hot oven—400° or more

The universal rule for good cooking might well be: have fresh things of the highest quality, prepared as simply as possible, and cooked at the last moment so that nothing sits around long. Specifics might include: scrub or scrape to clean, rather than peel vegetables, unless they have very tough skins. Bake rather than boil. Steam rather than boil. Boil briefly rather than fry. Stew or sauté in small amounts of water or oil rather than fry. Shred or slice thinly instead of cutting in large chunks. Add any seasoning or butter at the table, not on the stove. These are ways one learns as one goes along.

Every man is best satisfied with experiments made by himself; therefore I advise him who intends to practice, that he would repeat the trials of all mine before he relies upon them; not that I have been unfaithful in the making or relating any of them; nor doubt I but that, if he follow the same process his will succeed

as mine did, and he may very likely draw more inferences from
them than I have.   JETHRO TULL,
The Horse-Hoeing Husbandry, 1751

I have been asked which are the handiest tools I use
for cooking. First and foremost I would mention my
electric blender. For someone who professes and aspires
to simple living, this seems inconsistent and contradic-
tory. For twenty years in Vermont we lived happily
without electricity. When we moved to Maine we found
electricity connected to the old house we bought on a
back road. I received an electric blender as a gift,
scorned it, tried it a bit, found it an excellent tool to
soften up tough vegetables for soup, to make quick
drinks with overripe bananas, etc., etc. I now look on a
blender as very useful and the one thing I would miss if
we did not have electricity. Soups can be made in it in
minutes; vitamins and fuel and time can be saved. I
could live without a blender, but I sure use it a lot now
that I have one. When I mention to "whirl in blender,"
mashing or working through a sieve is the substitute.

Another handy electric gadget is a vegetable juicer.
We consume quantities of carrots, beets, celery and apples, put through our juicer, and the residues are used in
cooking. We have a little French grater for nuts and
seeds. It is a useful electric attachment.

Aside from these three exotic power-using tools, my
other kitchenware is usual and innocuous: wooden
spoons, bowls, sieves, scoops, lots of sharp knives, a large
skillet, a wok, a ten-quart soup kettle, a two-quart casserole.

My recipes will be used, I hope, as a whetstone for
further ventures in your own cooking. At best you will
like them and they will be good for you, and at least they

80

will be harmless and not hurt you. Any good recipes in this book should lead on to others of your own making. Convert and invent recipes of your own, and don't be averse to sharing and passing them on. Good recipes, like true love, are better given than bought.

A recipe doesn't belong to anyone. Given to me, I give it to you. It is only a guide, a skeletal framework. You must fill in the flesh according to your nature and desire.   EDWARD W. BROWN,
The Tassajara Bread Book, 1970

To Tasteful Palates, Keen Appetites, and Healthful and Capacious Stomachs the following Receipts composed for their Rational Recreation are respectfully inscribed. They have been written down by the fireside, with a spit in one hand, and a pen in the other.   DR. WILLIAM KITCHINER,
The Cook's Oracle, 1817

Ladies may now turn back their Sleeves, take off their rings and bracelets, and try for themselves.   LADY BARKER,
First Lessons in the Principles of Cooking, 1874

I THYNKE breakefastes necessary in this realme. Men and women not aged, havynge their stomackes cleane without putrified matter, slepynge moderately and soundly in the nyght, and feelinge them selve lyght in the morninge, and swete brethed, let them on goddis name breake their fast.

SIR THOMAS ELYOT,
The Castel of Helthe, 1534

Always breakfast as if you did not intend to dine, and dine as if you had not broken your fast.

DICK HUMELBERGIUS,
Tales of the Table, Kitchen & Larder, 1836

Let us rise early and fast, or break fast, gently and without perturbation.

HENRY DAVID THOREAU, *Walden*, 1854

To meet at the breakfast-table father, mother, children, all well, ought to be a happiness to any heart; it should be a source of humble gratitude, and should wake up the warmest feelings of our nature. Make it a rule never to come to the table in a churlish mood.

SOLON ROBINSON,
Facts for Farmers, 1866

The first duty of the mistress after breakfast is to give her orders for the day, and she naturally begins with the cook. On entering the kitchen, invariably say, "Good morning, cook" (a courtesy much appreciated below stairs).

ISABELLA M. BEETON,
Every-Day Cookery, 1872

It would be better at this meal that a visitor be given the alternative of taking a cup of tea in her room, and not appearing until luncheon.

M.E.W. SHERWOOD,
The Art of Entertaining, 1892

"Damn her!" Captain Huff said. "She swears to God she don't know how to cook, and I'm beginning to believe her. It's a disgrace to the town of Arundel and the whole damned province of Maine, if you ask me! Can't cook! Gosh! I never expected to live to see the day that a Maine woman couldn't cook!" "Mind your own business!" I told him. "There's plenty of women in Maine that can't cook, either, not any more than a chipmunk can, though they call it cooking. Why don't you cook your own breakfast?" KENNETH ROBERTS, *Arundel*, 1930

7

Break Fast with Breakfast?

*B*REAKFAST is a meal Scott and I can do without. At the most for us it is usually a cup of herb tea, of our own growing and drying, and a glass of rose hip juice, of our own growing and bottling. If we linger over the meal with talk amongst guests, we might serve bananas or apples, chew a handful of sunflower seeds, raisins or nuts. But usually before starting work in the morning we drink our herb tea with honey, and the rose hip juice for vitamin C. We feel lighter, brighter, more buoyant and brisker with this light repast.

> He felt as fresh as a two-tailed tadpole, strong and ready for anything, although he had not yet had a bite of breakfast. Or perhaps exactly on that account.   KURT ARNOLD FINDEISEN,
> *Abglanz des Lebens,* 1950

There have been times in our food experimentation (which we are always attempting) when we ate fruit only, and other times when we went without breakfast entirely, figuring the body had done nothing all night but rest, and needed the stimulus of some outdoor activity before it had earned the right to break its fast.

> It is right evydente to every wise man that to a man having due concoction and digestion as is expediente, shall in the mornynge fastynge, or with a lytell refection not onely have his intuecion quycker, his jugement perfecter, his tonge redyar, but also his reason fressher, his eare more attentife, his remembraunce more sure, and generally al his powers and wittis more effectuall and in better astate, than after he hath eate abundauntly.
>
> SIR THOMAS ELYOT,
> *The Boke Named the Govenour,* 1531

> The stomach needs time for rest, as well as any other muscular organ.
> WILLIAM A. ALCOTT,
> *The Young Housekeeper,* 1842

The body has utilized the sleeping period to assimilate the previous day's food, and does not need to be immediately plugged full again with food. With little energy having been expended throughout the night, the body's needs are nearly nil. The inner organs, particularly the stomach, can have sixteen hours on its own (from a six o'clock supper to noon lunch the next day) if no breakfast is taken. Breakfast is a good meal to skip.

Our theory is: the less food the better in life, as long as you get enough. You can train your body to expect and demand a big breakfast daily, or you can train it to accept little or nothing. No breakfast at all can become as much of a habit as eating a large amount of food with which to begin the day.

We agree with Thoreau who said, "The best breakfast is a breath of morning air and a long walk." Robert Louis Stevenson, writing on Thoreau, spoke of his abstinence from tea and coffee. "He thought it bad economy and worthy of no true virtuoso to spoil the natural rapture of the morning with such muddy stimulants."[1] Of Talley-rand, the French statesman of the late eighteenth century, Alexander Dumas said: "Dinner was the only meal he ate, for in the morning all he had before getting to work was three or four cups of camomile tea."

> It is remarkable, that notwithstanding the period which elapses between the meal of the previous day, and the hour of rising in the morning, there is generally little inclination to eat on first getting up from bed. This appears to arise from the condition of the stomach after a night's rest. This organ having during the night digested all the food remaining in it, probably falls in a state of quiescence; so that until the system is stimulated by exercise, or the stomach itself by food, hunger is not excited.
> SIR JOHN SINCLAIR,
> *The Code of Health and Longevity*, 1833

> Two meals a daye is suffycyent for a rest man; and a labourer maye eate thre tymes a day; and he that doth eate often lyveth a beestly lyfe. ANDREWE BOORDE,
> *A Dyetary of Helth*, 1542

Most people eat for breakfast what the neighbors eat. If they are French, they drink coffee and consume croissants; if British, porridge, bacon and eggs, and always coffee or tea; if Dutch, bread and slices of cheese and their milk-coffee. In India they may eat bananas and chappatis; in China, rice, and tea. Most Americans relish orange juice, toast and coffee, often with puffed, boxed cereals, easy to buy and to store and no effort to prepare. Custom and tradition dictate these breakfast habits.

> What more elegant breakfast can possibly be prepared—what more likely to raise the heart in thanksgiving to the bounteous Author of all good—than a basket or dish of strawberries, just

[1]Robert Louis Stevenson, *Men and Books*, 1888

from the native vines and stems, with all the richness of fragrance and deliciousness of taste, which in these circumstances cluster around them? And who is there, what with his mixed, heated, greasy breakfast, might not well envy (were envy ever admissable) his more fortunate neighbor, that can command for himself and his rising family, such simple, nutritious, cooling, wholesome and truly philosophic viands.

WILLIAM A. ALCOTT,
The Young Housekeeper, 1842

In our time we have feasted on one kind of fruit for meals pretty well all over the globe. In Singapore we've eaten all we could hold of ripe and dripping-sweet pineapples for a morning meal; in India, luscious mangoes or tiny finger-length bananas; in China on juicy persimmons; in southern France, on melons of all types; in South America on papayas. We have had cherries in Oregon and Washington states; peaches in Ohio; grapefruit or oranges or prunes or pears for breakfast in Florida and California. In New England we grow plenty of strawberries, raspberries and blackberries, which make fine breakfasts. But the prize fruit of all in our estimation, of which we never tire, is the apple. It does not cloy the taste. It is neither too sweet nor too sour. No matter how many you eat you can never get sick on them or of them.

To the individual of perfect appetite (though I do not yet know where such an individual can be found) the best way probably is to make a breakfast now and then of apples alone.

WILLIAM A. ALCOTT,
The Young Housekeeper, 1842

We aim at not mixing the fruits we eat. You can only eat so many peaches or strawberries at one sitting. Then you've had enough. You tend to overeat if you take a bit of one thing and then on to another or back to the first. Eat all you can or want of one thing and then stop. It is better for your weight as well as easier on the digestive system.

Although Scott and I usually carry on our morning's work with a cup or two of our herb tea drink until noon, I realize that we are country folk who stay at home from morning to night, day in and day out, and can have a solid lunch. Many of my readers may work at jobs that allow time for only a quick sandwich and a cup of something in the middle of the day. Their feeding situation must perforce be quite different than ours. So I am setting down some simple, hearty, homemade, harmless filler-ups for those whom Izaak Walton, in *The Compleat Angler* (1653), counsels to eat "a good, honest, wholesome, hungry breakfast."

POPCORN

Instead of buying cornflakes or any other of the boxed varieties of breakfast foods, why not try popcorn for a quick, easy, cheap breakfast? A big bowl of fresh popped corn, to be dipped into with one hand, and a good ripe banana in the other hand, combines to a fine and filling breakfast. And what could be easier for the cook, especially if someone else volunteers to pop the corn.

We buy a 50-pound bag of popcorn kernels wholesale, and can use up to two bags a year, as we serve popcorn on any occasion from breakfast to lunch to evening gatherings. One-pound bags or smaller cans of popcorn are available in most food stores.

The earliest way to pop corn was to put a cup of

kernels with a little oil in a heavy pan with a tight lid over a hot fire. The pan must be shaken back and forth to keep the kernels moving. It is not a long process. A friend of ours makes quick and easy popcorn this way in a large cast-aluminum pot on his electric stove. There are also long-handled wire baskets available, made just to pop corn over an open fire or stove. We have an electric corn popper which is very efficient. Melted butter and salt may be added to the corn just after it is popped, but we prefer it plain or with a little sea salt.

HORSE CHOW

In the early 1930s, before health foods and granola became household words, I made up a dish we called Horse Chow. At that time raw oats were not being eaten by humans. This is the simplest granola of all and perhaps one of the earliest. It was dreamed up in the Austrian Tyrol, where we holed up one winter in a village far from supplies and with a very slim larder of hit-or-miss articles, but with great appetites.

4 cups raw oats (old-fashioned, not the quick-cook kind)
½ cup raisins
Juice of 1 lemon
Dash of sea salt
Olive oil or vegetable oil to moisten

Mix all together. We eat it in wooden bowls with wooden spoons.

WHEAT BERRIES

Wheat berries is a prettier name than common ordinary wheat seed, which is all it is. It can be bought in health food stores or in a feed store (where it may have been treated with pesticides, so watch out). The ingredients are the simplest ever:

2 cups wheat seed, soaked overnight in
  a quart of water

In the morning, drain and drink the resulting elixir water, or feed it to your houseplants. Put the seeds in a kettle with enough water to cover by at least one inch, and let boil gently for up to 2 hours, adding more water as the seeds become absorbent.

On the back of my wood stove, the berries might cook up to 3 or 4 hours till they become tender. We eat them hot or cold, with honey, chopped apples or bananas, or (my favorite) a dash of olive oil and sea salt, or Scott's invention and daily addition to whatever grain is served at lunch.

SCOTT'S EMULSION

1 tablespoon honey
2 tablespoons peanut butter

Stir vigorously together into a smooth emulsion in your own bowl. (This is where the guest and eater has to do the work, not the cook.) Then fill your bowl with wheat berries (or kasha or millet). Again give all a good old stir and consume unlimited quantities.

MUESLI

One uncooked cereal dish that has become popular in the United States during the last decade was known in Europe years ago. We first came across it in the 1930s at the Bircher-Benner clinic in Zurich, Switzerland. When I made it at home in Vermont forty years ago, people liked it but couldn't pronounce its name: Bircher-Benner's Muesli. A facetious friend called the dish Bishop Brown's Mucilage. The original recipe called for soaking the rolled oats overnight, but I don't find that necessary.

2 cups raw oats (old-fashioned, not the quick-cook kind)
4 apples, unpeeled and grated
½ cup grated or chopped nuts or sunflower seeds
¼ cup raisins
1 tablespoon lemon juice (the grated rind can also be added)

Mix all together and eat immediately.

Variations: If sweetening is preferred, add a bit of honey or maple syrup, or moisten with a bit of apple juice or orange juice.

In those unholy days before we were responsible for inscribing our food-eating habits for posterity, sometimes for a birthday breakfast or special occasion we sweetened our muesli with a few spoonfuls of super-saturated-with-sugar condensed milk, and topped it with thinly sliced bananas, or with strawberries or raspberries or blueberries. When served for dessert our guests called it Apple Ice Cream. It is really too voluptuous for a breakfast food, unless for a once-a-year celebration.

MIRACLE MUSH

2 apples, unpeeled
1 carrot
1 beet, peeled
¼ cup grated nuts

Grate apples, carrot and beet and mix together. Sprinkle with grated nuts.

Variation: If too dry, moisten with some apple or orange juice.

DO-IT-YOURSELF GRANOLA

There are many granola recipes with a dozen or more ingredients. Here is a simple one.

3 cups rolled oats
3 cups rolled wheat
2 cups wheat germ
½ cup cut-up dates or dried apricots
1 cup chopped nuts
½ cup raisins

Mix all together, and store in a cool place or refrigerate. It can be browned in the oven until it is crunchy. When serving, some eat it with hot or cold milk.

Variation: You might add any one or more of the following: a teaspoon or two of sesame seeds, flax seeds, flaked coconut, brewers' yeast, pumpkin seeds, or even a dash of spices.

HOMINY GRITS

6 cups boiling water
3 cups ground cornmeal, soaked for an hour in water to cover
3 tablespoons butter
  Dash of sea salt
  Honey or maple syrup to taste

Add boiling water to soaked cornmeal and cook in double boiler till thick and smooth, about half an hour. Add butter, salt and honey or maple syrup. Serve hot.

Variation: Chopped or ground-up figs or dates may be added before serving.

SIMPLE BAKED CEREAL

1½ cups cornmeal
  2 cups rolled oats
  1 cup wheat germ
  1 cup grated coconut

½ cup vegetable oil
½ cup honey
1 teaspoon sea salt (optional)
1 cup water

Mix the dry ingredients together in a bowl, then add the wet. Spread on a large shallow pan and bake for half an hour. Put into individual bowls, and serve with honey and milk.

Variation: A small amount of sesame seeds, raisins and chopped dates may be added.

HEARTY BARLEY

Soak 1 cup barley overnight in a quart of water. In morning, bring to a boil, then cook slowly for 15 minutes. Drain off any excess water and save same for soup stock. Serve with honey or maple syrup. This can also be eaten cold for a dessert, with cream and more sweetening.

BROSE

This Scotch "stirabout" is not cooked at all. It is made by pouring boiling water on oatmeal and stirring briskly till thick and smooth. Use as much oatmeal and as much boiling water as will bring it to the thickness required. When hot soup stock or butter or oil is added instead of boiling water, it is called Fat Brose in Scotland, and Budram if the hot cereal is turned into cups or small molds and eaten cold.

Whether Brose or Budram, it is good with honey, maple syrup and milk.

BREAKFAST WARMER

1 cup cracked wheat or bulgur
1 apple, chopped
4 tablespoons butter
½ cup shelled nuts
½ cup raisins

Bring 4 cups water to a rapid boil. Add the wheat gradually while stirring. Simmer for 15 to 20 minutes, only till wheat is chewable. Do not overcook. Remove from the stove and add, stirring, the apple, butter, nuts and raisins.

SUPER CEREAL

2 cups cracked wheat or bulgur
6 dates, chopped
2 tablespoons sunflower seeds
2 tablespoons sesame seeds
1 ripe banana, sliced
   Honey or maple syrup or applesauce, optional

Stir the bulgur into 3 cups cold water and stir until smooth. Cook over low heat for 15 to 20 minutes, stirring frequently. Take off stove and add dates, seeds, and banana. Sweeten as and if desired with honey or maple syrup. If too dry, I have stirred in some applesauce.

OLD SOAK CEREAL

½ cup millet
½ cup rolled oats
½ cup buckwheat groats
1 cup raisins
2 tablespoons butter
¼ cup sunflower seeds
   Honey or maple syrup

Soak the above ingredients overnight in ample water to cover. In morning bring to a boil, adding more water if needed. If kept just at boiling point, the grains will stay separate and not gum up. Add a dab of butter and a handful of sunflower seeds on serving, with honey or maple syrup to taste.

*T*HE herbes with the whiche potage is made withall, yf they be pure, good, and clene, not worme-eaten, nor infected with the corrupte ayre descendynge upon them, doth comfort many men. A grewell made with otmel and herbes can do lytel displeasure and relaxeth ye belly.

ANDREWE BOORDE, *A Dyetary of Helth*, 1542

Soup is within the reach of every housekeeper, and is even accessible to the lower orders of the people, and when once tried, it will be found that there cannot be a greater luxury that will go twice as far in a family.

ANONYMOUS, *How a Small Income Suffices*, 1745

What a relief to the labouring husband to have a warm comfortable soup!

MARIA ELIZA RUNDELL,
A New System of Domestic Cookery, 1807

At Lady Blessington's dinner party the soup vanished in the busy silence that beseems it.   NATHANIEL PARKER WILLIS, *Life Here and There*, 1850

On the score of economy, we say, have soup every day. On the score of health, we say, have soup every day.   ANONYMOUS, *Table Observances*, 1854

The uneasiness of hunger can be more quicky removed by a bowl of good soup than by any other variety of food.   J.B. & L.E. LYMAN,
How to Live, 1882

I am sorry to say that more American housekeepers can make delicate and rich cake than excellent soups.   MARION HARLAND,
Cookery for Beginners, 1884

We hold that soup will always act beneficially, provided it be good.

J.L.W. THUDICUM, *The Spirit of Cookery*, 1895

Hearing a good loud soup is very enjoyable.

BERT MILTON, *How to Behave at a Banquet*, 1912

To possess a cook who makes perfect soups is to possess a jewel of great price. A woman who cannot make soup should not be allowed to marry.

P. MORTON SHAND, *A Book of Food*, 1928

8

Soups & Soups & Soups

A partiality for soups has kept me, and probably always will keep me, from the true-believers' ranks of raw-fooders. Both my parents came from European stock, where soup tureens were on every table. They brought up their family to a liking for soup, and a serving of them once a day. It is a habit I have continued since my own housekeeping days began. In fact, my fame, if fame there be as a cook, is based largely upon soups I made up for the multitudes who streamed into our country place and usually stayed for a meal. I seem to put soups together acceptably. And to my mind, it is the one thing that I as a cook can do well occasionally.

> Make a good soup, a distinctive soup, a soup your friends can rely upon, and you're a chef. *Esquire's Handbook for Hosts,* 1949

Soup is a comforting dish, easily concocted, easily digested, and universally acceptable. Soups can be very cheap, using up many odds and ends from earlier meals.

They can be a happy home for leftovers and vegetable water. A bit of this root vegetable, a leaf or two of that green, an herb or two, some odd bits left from the day before, add water, and you have it. In creating a soup I find it one-third products on hand, one-third ingenuity to do with what is available, and one-third good luck.

I never know what one of my soups will taste like because I am always adding new leftovers. Sometimes I make a really good soup (usually of scrap ingredients) and then, like the Lost Chord in music, can never find it again. What went into it to make it unusually good? Some forgotten ingredient that added a magical something. Many have asked me and received no acceptable answer: "What went *into* this soup? I've used everything you've mentioned, but *my* soup doesn't turn out this way."

I can only say that my soups are often a surprise to me. They are sometimes very good, sometimes not so, but always filling and nourishing. There is no clean scrap of any edible substance too insignificant for use in the soup kettle. I don't "make" a soup; it makes itself from what is growing in the garden at that time, from what is dried in the pantry, from what is left over from the days before, from what is preserved in the cellar. A well-stocked pantry and a thriving kitchen garden makes soup-making easy for the cook and exceedingly cheap.

Soup has other advantages. It takes the edge off the appetite so that the lack of other items on the table is not so noticeable. It can be made in advance and reheated. With a good fire and hardly any notice one can feed a small multitude with a big pot of soup. I have proven this again and again when a crowd of anywhere from half a dozen to a score of people drop in unannounced. For six months a year Scott and I are blissfully alone. For six

months a year (May to October) I feed all and sundry—
sometimes as many as twenty-seven to a meal. Soup is
my life-saver.

Today, with food fantastically high in price, a good soup, a useful
soup, can be the backbone of your meal.   MARIE A. ESSIPOFF,
                    Making the Most of Your Cooking Time, 1952

Given a cook of good instincts and gay imagination, and from one
year's end to the other, never need the same soup be served a
second time. . . . Equally desirable in illness and in health, during
one's journeys abroad and one's days at home, why is it that soup
has never yet been praised and glorified as it should?
                         ELIZABETH ROBBINS PENNELL,
                             A Guide for the Greedy, 1896

There are various kinds of excellent soups suited to each season
of the year, which frugal families, chiefly in the country, who
know how to live comfortably on a small income, generally make
a part of their food three or four times a week, adding some little
article according to their circumstances, and varying the kind of
soup by way of change.   ANONYMOUS,
                     How a Small Income Suffices, 1745

There is no more wholesome, nutritious and economic food than
soup—for a family, low or high. Soup should be used in every
family, and especially by working-folk. A French, Swiss or German peasant farmer has soup on his table every day, and often
twice. Without soup his world would come to an end.
                              JOHN T. WALTERS,
                                  Thrift Lessons, 1881

Soups can be made out of almost anything and almost out of nothing. A tale I read long ago tells of an
ingenious Stone Soup. A wandering tramp in France
approached a country housewife's cottage and asked to
borrow a kettle so he could make some soup for himself. She asked if he had the ingredients, and he replied
that he had a stone. Mystified, she exclaimed, "You

can't make soup out of a stone." "Oh, yes," he said, "I'll just show you if you will lend me the kettle and let me have some water." She did so gladly and he set to, making a fire. He put the well-washed stone in the bottom of the kettle while the water was heating. Then he asked, "Now, you wouldn't mind letting me have a sprig of sage from your herb garden?" No, she'd let him have that. "And a bit of dandelion weeds growing around your doorstep?" That too was allowed. He kept on filching an odd herb here and a leaf there while she watched him and while the water bubbled. He found some dried pods and extracted the seeds. She began to understand his "stone" soup when he asked if she didn't have a small potato lying around and maybe an old bone. All these things went into the kettle where his stone lay heating. Finally he said, "Voilà! My soup is ready. Will you taste it?" And he had made a satisfactory soup with his stone base.

There is one thing about a good soup. It must be either very hot or it must be chilled. There is nothing worse than a lukewarm soup.

> A young waiter brought a bowl of soup to the table in a restaurant. Before he could set it down, the diner said: "Boy, take that soup right back to the kitchen. It is lukewarm." "But," the astonished waiter said, "you haven't even tried it yet." "That's right," said the enraged customer. "But it's not necessary. If your thumb can take it, it's not hot enough."   M.E.W. SHERWOOD,
> *The Art of Entertaining*, 1892

Soups can be made exceedingly rich and thick, or can be watery broth. Robert Louis Stevenson has a Scotch lord say in *The Master of Ballantrae* (1899): "I think these broth would be better to sweem in than to sup."

Make your soups neither too thick nor yet too thin. A contemporary John Keats has put it well: "Consistency too thin to plow and too thick to drink."[1]

There is a story of Alfred Tennyson who as a small boy tried the soup his father served at table. "Oh, father," he is said to have enthused. "That's a rare good soup." His puritanical father, after tasting it, said, "You're right, bairn. It's *too* good," and thinned it down with the water from his tumbler.

Thinning soups is easy. I often have to add water or tomato juice to soup when I feed more of a crowd than I expected. To thicken, I have made a paste of flour and cold water, stirring this mixture into the hot soup. I have also thrown in finely ground nuts, and even grated a raw potato to quickly add bulk. Adding a grated raw carrot at the last minute gives a rich color and adds flavor and texture to some soups. An apple, shredded, or a mashed boiled potato, serves to thicken beet borscht.

If salt is added to soups, do not boil it with the vegetables for a long time. Add it within a few minutes of taking soup off the stove. If soups are too salty, add a halved raw potato and boil for a few minutes. The potato will absorb the salt and can be taken out before serving.

If you want to add croutons to some soups and no dried breadcrumbs are available, try puffed rice or wheat that has been crisped in the oven, or popcorn.

Garnish soups with finely chopped blades of wheat grass or chopped leaves of young comfrey. Raw cabbage or young onion or parsley, finely chopped, and thrown in at the last few minutes of cooking, can revivify and

[1]In *The Artist's & Writer's Cook Book,* 1961

add life to a tired two- or three-day-old soup. Sprinkle with alfalfa sprouts or finely sliced raw celery or green pepper instead of the more traditional parsley or chives or green onion tops. Add a squeeze of lemon and a lemon slice to black bean soup.

If a soup lacks zing or zest, I've been known to throw a can of boughten tomato juice into the soup pot to add flavor and volume when suddenly more was needed. One of my more captious critics, on hearing this, said, "I hope you open the can first, Helen."

I have heard that stirring a thick vegetable soup with a knife that has been used to cut a clove of garlic will add flavor, or rubbing the cut surface of a garlic bud over the bottom of the individual soup bowl before pouring in the hot liquid. The princess who felt the pea under ten mattresses might sense this barely tangible flavor; I am less cautious in its use. A chopped-up clove or two goes into many of my soups.

The shallot does not assert itself with the fury and pertinacity of garlic; it does not announce its presence with the self-consciousness of the onion. It appeals by more refined devices, by gentler means, and is to be prized accordingly.

ELIZABETH ROBBINS PENNELL,
A Guide for the Greedy, 1896

When meat savour is impossible, or is intentionally withheld, the craving for taste has to be satisfied by strong vegetable flavour, and the acceptable substance selected to that end is the onion. Hence those strongly-flavoured meals which surround men with a tainted atmosphere, and cause them to be avoided by sensitive persons. Such feeding is only fit for persons who remain in quarantine or the open air, and its results should not be inflicted upon aesthetical noses. The soups and vegetable dishes consisting mainly of onions should be mitigated, so as to be adapted to polite intercourse.

J.L.W. THUDICUM,
The Spirit of Cookery, 1895

To my mind, every good soup begins with an onion, chopped and simmered in oil. A good brown soup can be made by sautéeing onion or garlic in oil, with chopped vegetables and herbs added till the fat is absorbed and the vegetables browned. Boiling water is then poured on (about three times as much liquid as vegetables) and your soup or broth emerges. Any combination of vegetables or herbs or vegetable stock water can be used. Such secrets of soups as I have are: onions first and onions last. Start with them, sautéeing as you cut up other vegetables, and end by scattering chopped onions, raw, into the soup five minutes before serving.

> In making any kind of soups set the pan on a very slow fire, with onions, herbs and roots cut small, with a large lump of butter. This will draw all the virtue out of the different ingredients, will produce a good gravy, and a very different effect, in point of flavour, than if at first you had put in water. Fill your pan with water as soon as the onions are browned, and then follow the directions for making the sort of soup you wish to have.
>
> FREDERIC NUTT,
> *The Important & Royal Cook,* 1809

I use my blender almost daily to make raw or lightly cooked soups. The less the cooking, the fewer vitamins are lost, so I tend to undercook and then throw the vegetables into the blender: a whirl of this, a toss of that in some vegetable juice, and a soup is ready to reheat or to sip cold. Spinach, celery, boiled potatoes, tomatoes, any soft vegetable can be made into a purée in a few seconds. Even leftover salads can be put in the blender with some vegetable juice and make a savory soup, or be added to existing soups.

My German grandmother, I remember, always started soup in *cold* water, to get the flavor out of the vegetables. Cooked vegetables she put in *boiling* water, to seal the flavor in—to conserve their goodness.

Let the materials be what they may, they should be put over the fire in cold water, and kept at a low temperature for the first hour, at least. The chief secret in the, to many, occult art of soup-brewing is steady slow cooking for a long time. To be hasty in the process is to mar. Impatience but accelerates ruin. For two hours the contents of the pot should simmer drowsily beneath a closely fitting lid. Then the heat may be increased until a gentle bubble agitates the liquid. From the beginning to the end of the operation nothing is gained and much imperilled by a 'good hard boil.'   MARION HARLAND,
The Cottage Kitchen, 1883

Causing anything to boil violently in any culinary process is very ill judged . . . if it were possible to keep the soup always just boiling hot, without actually boiling, it would be so much the better.   COUNT RUMFORD,
Essays on Feeding the Poor, 1798

Let the soup be very slowly heated, and after it has boiled for a few minutes, draw it to the side of the stove and keep it simmering softly, but without ceasing, until it is done; for on this its excellence depends. Every good cook understands perfectly the difference produced by the fast boiling or the gentle stewing of soups and gravies, and will adhere strictly to the latter method.
ELIZA ACTON,
Modern Cookery for Private Families, 1845

"To make good soup, the pot should scarcely smile," said a Frenchman, which, in less poetic terms, means: start in cold water and slowly bring to the boil so that the juices may be drawn out.

This long, slow cooking, which imparts full flavor to soups, is no extra trouble with a wood stove. On the contrary, much can be done elsewhere in the house or outside while the soup is taking care of itself, instead of at the last minute making a rousing fire and watching a heavily boiling pot. I have done hours of outside masonry work, without a thought to lunch, and come in at noon to find soup for half a dozen fellow-workers ready on the stove and cooked to a turn.

Soups can better with age. A first-day soup may be a try-out, an experiment. The second day it may be better. Often by the third day it is mellowed and at its peak. It can hardly improve after that through thinning or thickening, though our modern refrigeration can keep it fresh and edible for days.

Prepare your broths and soups the evening before you want them. This will give you more time to attend to the rest of your dinner the next day.   MRS. N.K.M. LEE,
The Cook's Own Book, 1832

When soups or gravies are to be put by, let them be changed every day into fresh scalded pots.   THOMAS COOPER,
A Practical System of Domestic Cookery, 1824

This last warning is very useful when a big soup has not all been consumed. It may last for three or four days, and while soups may get better with age, there is a point at which they may turn sour. So, clean kettles and one good hard boiling shortly before serving is wise.

Soup can be a meal in itself or a light start to the meal. In polite society the soup is only a prelude to the meal —the preface of a dinner, but that is not always understood by less sophisticated, country folk.

Scott has told me the story of a countryman from a rural community who was elected to high office and sent to Washington. He attended a great dinner party and very much relished the first dish served him. He sent his bowl back seven times (so Scott says, though it is hard to believe) for more of the delicious soup. "And then," sighed the congressman, "they brought on the

105

best dinner I ever did see and there I sat chock-full of soup."

If the hostess wishes full justice to be done to the remainder of her dinner, she will not begin by giving her guests a thick soup. The real function of soup is gently to stimulate rather than to satisfy the appetite. Thick soup takes away the appetite and the tantalized guest sees course after course of dishes pass him by, while he is aware of his incapacity to do them justice.

ANONYMOUS,
The Young Ladies' Treasure Book, 1885

In the French provinces, the country people and the farmers still call the evening meal La Soupe because it is made up of little else.
CLAIRE DE PRATZ,
French Home Cooking, 1856

There are those who believe no good soup can be made without a meat stock. This, of course, is not true, as I and thousands of other vegetarians have demonstrated day after day. The water in which all vegetables are boiled may be saved for soup stock. Save the liquid in which beans or wheat or lentils have soaked overnight. Keep the outside stalks and leaves of celery, raw potato peelings, coarse cabbage or lettuce leaves, stems of broccoli or kale or asparagus, spinach leaves, overripe tomatoes, coarse green tops of leeks and onions. Wash and cut, cover with cold water, and simmer for at least an hour, then sieve. According to season, use onions, sliced carrots, rutabaga, turnip, celeriac, lovage leaves, basil, thyme, sage, summer savory, or other fresh or dried herbs. A spray of lemon juice brightens a soup stock, or a bay leaf.

Get Chervil, Beets, Chards, Spinach, Sellery, Leeks and such like Herbs, with two or three large Crusts of Bread, some Butter, a

bunch of Sweet-herbs, and a little Salt; put these, with a moderate Quantity of Water, into a Kettle, and boil them for an Hour and a half, and strain out the Liquor through a Sieve, and it will be a good Stock for Soups. ANONYMOUS,
The Lady's Companion, 1753

No family who can afford a kitchen at all, is too poor to be without a stock-pot. LADY BARKER,
Houses & Housekeeping, 1876

In a passage of Cicero he says, "Except hot broth, my cook can do nothing cleverly." Perhaps I was Cicero's cook in an earlier incarnation. Even now it is about all I am good for in the cooking line. I enjoy making up soups. Maybe that is why they are better than most of my cooking.

The art of composing a rich soup is so to proportion the several ingredients one to another that no particular taste be stronger than the rest, but to produce such a fine harmonious relish that the whole is delightful. This requires that judicious combination of the materials which constitutes the chef d'oeuvre of culinary science. MRS. N.K.M. LEE,
The Cook's Own Book, 1832

EVERYDAY VEGETABLE SOUP

2–3	tablespoons butter or oil
3	onions, chopped
4	potatoes, peeled and diced
4	carrots, thinly sliced
2	turnips, diced
¼	head cabbage, shredded or chopped
4	cups tomato juice
1	cup chopped fresh parsley or chives

Heat the butter or oil in a large kettle, and sauté the onions until tender. Add the vegetables, along with enough water to cover. Simmer the mixture until the potatoes and turnips are tender—about half an hour. Add the tomato juice, and continue cooking until it is heated through. Add the chopped parsley or chives, and serve.

Variation: To make a creamy vegetable soup, sauté the onions as directed above. Purée the chopped vegetables with the stock (one-half at a time) in a blender, and add the mixture to the onions. Cook for half an hour. Season with a dash of soy sauce, and sprinkle with the parsley just before serving.

SIMPLE SUMMER SOUP

This is a light and refreshing warm-weather soup. For an interesting variation, add a pint of frozen peas, barely thawed, to the soup just before serving.

1   pint plain yogurt
2   cups tomato juice
    Juice of 1 orange
    Few mint leaves

Blend the yogurt and tomato juice. Add the orange juice and mint leaves. Serve the soup well chilled.

SPRINGTIME SOUP

As green as the first leaves of spring, this soup is a delightful way to welcome the new season.

2–3 tablespoons butter or oil
2 bunches scallions, chopped
2 young carrots, thinly sliced
2 cups fresh peas
A few stalks of asparagus, cut into ½" pieces
Handful of green celery leaves or lovage or spinach, chopped
6 cups stock or water

Heat the butter or oil in a large skillet, and sauté the scallions and carrots for a few minutes. Add the peas, asparagus and green leaves, and cook, stirring. Meanwhile, heat the stock or water in a large kettle; when hot, add the vegetables and bring to a boil. Cover the kettle, and simmer the soup for 15 to 20 minutes.

AUTUMN SOUP

Who said good soup has to cook all day? This one is done quickly because this time I start with boiling water.

1 cup finely shredded cabbage
1 cup chopped celery
1 cup chopped broccoli
½ cup chopped parsley
4 cups boiling water (approximately)
Dash of soy sauce or vegetable salt or lemon juice

Put the vegetables in a pot, and add the boiling water. Add the soy sauce or salt or lemon juice. Cover the pot, and cook for half an hour.

SIMPLEST SOUP OF ALL

4–6 potatoes, unpeeled
2–3 tablespoons butter
    Sea salt to taste
  ½ cup chopped parsley

Scrub the potatoes, and cut them into chunks. Place them in a pot, and add enough cold water to cover. Bring to a boil, and cook until fork-tender—about 20 minutes. Churn the potatoes in a blender, adding a little water if necessary. Reheat. Serve with the butter, sea salt and parsley.

COLD VEGETABLE SOUP

2 cups chopped onions or leeks
1 cup chopped celery
4 cups tomato juice
1 tablespoon soy sauce
2 cups water
  Handful fresh parsley, chopped

Churn all the ingredients—except the parsley—one-half at a time in the blender. Transfer the mixture to a saucepan, and heat to a low temperature. Bring to a quick boil and immediately take off heat. Chill the soup well, and serve garnished with the parsley.

CHINESE THIN SOUP

10 small garlic cloves, chopped
1   bunch scallions, chopped
2   tablespoons soy sauce
1   tablespoon sesame oil
1   teaspoon sea salt
7   cups boiling water

Place the garlic, scallions, soy sauce, sesame oil and sea salt in a medium saucepan. Pour the boiling water over all, and cook for 10 minutes.

TOMATO SOUP

2–3 tablespoons butter or oil
2   onions, chopped
1   pound tomatoes, chopped
2   quarts water
1   bay leaf
     Pinch of sea salt
½   cup chopped green pepper or parsley

Heat the butter or oil in a large skillet, and sauté the onions until soft. Add the tomatoes and continue cooking. Meanwhile, boil the water in a large kettle. Add the tomato mixture to the kettle, along with the remaining ingredients. Simmer for 15 minutes. Just before serving, remove and discard the bay leaf.

RAW TOMATO SOUP

6   ripe tomatoes, quartered
1   green onion, chopped
3   tablespoons olive oil
2   cups water
     Fresh basil or oregano leaves to taste
     Chopped chives or parsley

Churn all the ingredients, one-half at a time, in a blender until smooth. Transfer the mixture to a serving bowl, and serve chilled. Garnish with chopped chives or parsley.

SIMPLE ONION SOUP

½   cup butter or oil
6   onions, sliced
2   cloves garlic, chopped
½   cup soy sauce
6   cups water
     Handful of fresh sorrel leaves, chopped

Heat the oil or butter in a large skillet, and add the onions. Cook slowly over low heat until onions are tender. Add the garlic and soy sauce. Boil the water in a large kettle, then add the onion mixture, along with the sorrel leaves. Cover the kettle, and simmer on low heat for 15 or 20 minutes.

Variation: Leeks can be used instead of onions.

SPANISH SOUP

This is also called gazpacho; in any language, it tastes great on a hot day.

4   tomatoes, quartered
2   cucumbers, peeled and chopped
1   onion, chopped
2   cloves garlic, chopped
1   green pepper, chopped
1   tablespoon olive oil
½   teaspoon cumin
1   tablespoon fresh basil leaves, chopped
    Black olives, chopped
    Dry bread cubes

Combine all the ingredients (except the garnish), one-half at a time, in a blender; whirl for a very short time so that the texture is not too smooth. Serve the soup well chilled in individual bowls, garnished with black olives and dry bread cubes.

CARROT SOUP

2   tablespoons butter
2   cups shredded carrots
1   cup sliced celery
1   onion, chopped
3   tomatoes, quartered
1   cup boiling water
4   cups tomato juice

Melt the butter in a heavy pot, and add the vegetables. Sauté the vegetables just until they start to brown. Add the boiling water; cover the pot and simmer until the vegetables are tender—about 15 minutes. Add the tomato juice, and continue cooking until it is heated through.

SIMPLE CELERY SOUP

As in the other recipes, if you use stock instead of water for the cooking liquid, the soup will have a more full-bodied flavor.

1	head celery
2–3	tablespoons butter or oil
1	potato, scrubbed and chopped
4	cups stock or water
	Pinch of sea salt
	Pinch of nutmeg

Remove the celery hearts and save them to use in salads. Chop the remaining celery, including the leaves. Set the leaves aside for garnish. Heat the butter or oil in a medium saucepan, and sauté the celery and potato. Add the stock or water, and bring to a boil. Simmer for 45 minutes, or until the celery is soft. Add the sea salt and the nutmeg, and garnish with the chopped celery leaves just before serving.

Variation: For a creamy celery soup, cook the soup as directed above; put it through a mill or sieve, or blend it coarsely, adding more water if desired.

FRESH PEA SOUP

1 quart fresh green peas, shelled
6 green onions, chopped

Set aside a handful of the youngest peas to use as a garnish. Place the remaining peas in a medium saucepan, and add enough boiling water to cover. Add the chopped onions, and bring to a boil again. Purée the mixture, one-half at a time, in a blender, adding a little more water if necessary. Reheat the soup, and serve with the baby peas floating on top.

DRIED MUSHROOM SOUP

8 dried mushrooms, washed and soaked in hot water until soft
2 tablespoons butter or oil
2 onions, sliced
½ cup barley, soaked overnight in ample water to cover
1 potato, peeled and cubed
¼ teaspoon cumin seeds
2 tablespoons soy sauce
1 teaspoon sea salt
4 cups water

Cut the mushrooms into small pieces. Heat the butter or oil in a saucepan, and sauté the mushrooms and onions until tender. Add the remaining ingredients. Cover the saucepan and simmer for a full hour.

FRESH MUSHROOM SOUP

¼ cup butter or oil
1 cup finely chopped celery
1 cup finely chopped onions
1 cup finely chopped leeks
1 cup finely chopped fresh mushrooms
1–2 tablespoons flour
2 or more cups vegetable stock

Heat the butter or oil in a wok or medium saucepan, and add the celery, sautéeing until transparent, then the onions and leeks. When these are slightly tender, add the mushrooms and mix together for a few minutes. Simmer over low heat until the vegetables are tender. Stir in the flour, blending until smooth. Add enough vegetable stock to obtain desired consistency —less if you want a really thick soup, more if you want to stretch it further. Simmer the soup for 15 minutes.

LEEK SOUP

3 tablespoons butter
6 leeks, cut into 2″ pieces
2 potatoes, peeled and thinly sliced
4 cups water
¼ cup chopped parsley
Dash of soy sauce

Melt 2 tablespoons of the butter in a medium saucepan, and gently cook the leeks over low heat. Add the

116

potatoes and water, and simmer for 1 hour. Just before serving, add the remaining butter, parsley and soy sauce.

POTATO SOUP

10	potatoes, scrubbed, peeled and diced
2–3	tablespoons butter or oil
2	onions, chopped
	Pinch of garlic powder
	Pinch of dill seed or celery seed
	Pinch of sea salt
¼	cup chopped parsley

Place the potatoes in a large kettle with enough cold water to cover them. Bring to a boil and cook until tender—about 15 minutes. Meanwhile, heat the butter or oil in a medium skillet, and sauté the onions until soft. Add the onions to the potatoes, along with the seasonings. Simmer for 15 to 20 minutes. Serve garnished with the chopped parsley.

Variation: For a creamy soup, this mixture can be blended just before serving, and reheated.

SIMPLEST BARLEY SOUP

2	tablespoons butter or oil
4	onions, sliced
1½	cups barley, soaked overnight in ample water to cover
	A generous pinch of dried thyme
	Dash of soy sauce

Heat the butter or oil in a large skillet, and sauté the onions until soft. Add the barley and its water if any, and stir in the dried thyme. Transfer to a large kettle, and add enough boiling water to cover. Cook for an hour, adding more water if necessary. Just before serving, add the soy sauce.

WINTER SOUP

Hearty and flavorful.

½   cup barley, soaked overnight in 4 cups cold water
2   tablespoons butter or oil
2   stalks celery, chopped
2   carrots, diced
2   potatoes, peeled and cubed
2   onions, chopped
2   leeks, sliced
    Handful of tender kale leaves, chopped
¼   cup butter or sour cream
    Pinch of nutmeg

Cook the barley and water until tender—a full hour. Meanwhile, heat the 2 tablespoons of butter or oil in a large skillet, and sauté the celery, carrots, potatoes, onions and leeks until tender. Add the vegetables to the barley mixture, along with additional boiling water if a thinner soup is desired. Cook for 5 minutes. Add the kale and simmer for 15 minutes. Just before serving, add the butter or sour cream and the nutmeg.

RAW BEET BORSCHT

2 cups diced raw beets
1 green onion, chopped
2 cups sour cream or plain yogurt
Pinch of caraway seed
Sea salt to taste

Place half the beets, onion and sour cream or yogurt in a blender, and liquefy; repeat with the remaining beets, onion and sour cream or yogurt. Add caraway and sea salt to taste. Serve well chilled.

BEET BORSCHT

4 cups shredded raw beets
1 onion, finely chopped
4 cups stock or tomato juice
Juice of ½ lemon
½ teaspoon sea salt
2 tablespoons soy sauce
½ cup sour cream

Place the beets, onion and stock in a large kettle. Bring to a boil and simmer for half an hour. Add the lemon juice, salt, and soy sauce. Serve hot or cold, with dabs of sour cream. Serves 6.

Variation: Instead of lemon juice, add 1 cup orange juice.

ROSE HIP SOUP

4 cups rose hip purée (see instructions on pages 286–87)
6 cardamom seeds, finely ground
2 tablespoons maple syrup
¼ cup ground almonds
¼ cup raisins
   Dash of nutmeg
1 cup water

Combine all ingredients but the raisins, one half at a time, in the blender, and churn until smooth. Add raisins. Serve hot or cold. (If to be heated, do not boil.)

SIMPLE LENTIL SOUP

1 cup dried lentils
2 onions, chopped
2 cloves garlic, chopped
1 bay leaf
2 quarts water
   Grated peel of 1 lemon

Combine all ingredients in a medium saucepan and gently simmer for an hour, or until the lentils are tender. Serves 6.

PARTY LENTIL SOUP

2 cups dried lentils and ample water to cover
2–3 tablespoons butter or oil
2 onions, chopped
4 stalks celery, chopped
2 cloves garlic, minced
4 cups stock or water
½ teaspoon ground cumin
½ teaspoon ground coriander
Pinch of curry powder
Pinch of sea salt
Grated peel of 1 lemon

Place the lentils in a large kettle and add enough water to cover them. Bring to boiling; lower the heat, and simmer for half an hour. Meanwhile, heat the butter or oil in a large skillet, and sauté the onions, celery and garlic until soft. Add the vegetables and the seasonings to the lentils, along with the stock or water, and bring to a boil. Lower the heat, cover the kettle, and simmer an hour or longer. Serves 8.

Variation: For a creamy lentil soup, purée in a blender, adding water if necessary.

HEARTY BLACK BEAN SOUP

2 cups dried black beans, soaked in 8 cups of water overnight in a large kettle
1 bay leaf
3 tablespoons butter or oil

2 onions, chopped
2 stalks celery, sliced
2 carrots, diced
2 cloves garlic, minced
1 tablespoon lemon juice
½ teaspoon cumin seed
½ teaspoon oregano
4 cups tomato juice

Bring the beans, the bay leaf and the water to a boil; lower the heat and simmer until the beans are soft—a full hour. Meanwhile, heat the butter or oil in a large skillet, and add the onions, celery, carrots and garlic; stew over low heat for 10 minutes or until tender. When the beans are soft, add the vegetables to the kettle, along with the lemon juice, seasonings and the tomato juice. Bring to a boil, discard the bay leaf, and serve. Serves 8.

DRIED PEA SOUP

2 cups dried peas, soaked in 2 quarts cold water overnight
2 cups chopped celery
1 tablespoon celery seed
1 teaspoon sea salt
  A few mint leaves
2 tablespoons butter

Cook the peas in water until the peas are tender—about an hour. Remove the kettle from the heat, and add the celery and seasonings. Purée the mixture, one-half at a time, in the blender until smooth. Reheat the soup. Just before serving, add the butter. Serves 6 to 8.

COUNTRY SOUP

1   cup dried lima beans and 1 cup dried kidney beans,
    soaked overnight in ample water to cover
3   carrots, sliced
1   onion, sliced
1   clove garlic, minced
1   head celery, chopped (reserve hearts for salad)
2   tomatoes, quartered
4   cups water
1   teaspoon dried mint leaves

Cook the beans in water over low heat until they are tender—about 1 ½–2 hours. Add the vegetables to the beans, along with the water, and cook until the celery is tender—about 30 minutes. During the last 10 minutes of cooking, add the mint leaves. Serves 6.

SUPER SUPPER SOUP

1   cup any type of dried beans, soaked overnight in
    2 quarts cold water
2–3 tablespoons butter or oil
2   onions or leeks, sliced
2   potatoes, scrubbed and cubed
2   stalks celery, sliced
3   carrots, sliced
2   turnips, cubed
1   clove garlic, minced
    Pinch each of thyme, marjoram, aniseed

Bring the beans and water to a boil; lower the heat and simmer until the beans are soft—about an hour. In a large skillet, heat the butter or oil, and sauté the vegetables until they are soft. Add the vegetables to the beans, along with the seasonings; simmer 30 minutes. Serves 6 to 8.

FAVA BEAN SOUP

4 tablespoons butter or oil
1 onion, chopped
2 cups dried fava beans, soaked overnight in ample cold water to cover
1 cup chopped celery
2 quarts water
2 tomatoes, coarsely chopped
1 teaspoon oregano

Heat 2 tablespoons of the butter or oil in a large kettle, and sauté the onions until soft. Add the beans, celery and water; simmer until the beans are tender—about 1 hour. In a small skillet, heat the remaining butter or oil, and sauté the tomatoes. Add the tomatoes and oregano to the beans. Bring to a boil, and serve. Serves 6 to 8.

CREAMY BLUEBERRY SOUP

1 pint blueberries
2 cups water
½ cup maple syrup
½ teaspoon cinnamon

1   pinch cardamom
1   cup sour cream

Wash the blueberries and place them in a saucepan with the water, maple syrup, cinnamon and cardamom. Cook slowly for 15 minutes; remove from heat and let cool. Stir in the sour cream, and chill well before serving.

*T*AKE parsley, sage, garlic, onions, leek, borage, cresses, rue, rosemary and purslain. Lave them and wash them clean. Pluck them small with thy hand and mix them well with raw oil. Lay on vinegar and salt and serve it forth. SAMUEL PEGGE, *The Forme of Cury,* 1390

Among al herbest, non hath so good juyce as lettyse. It doth sette a hotte stomake in a very good temper, maketh good appetite, and eaten in the evenynge provoketh slepe. It provoketh mylke in a womans breastes, but it abateth carnall appetite. SIR THOMAS ELYOT,
The Castel of Helthe, 1534

First then to speak of Sallets, there be some simple and some compounded; some only to furnish out the table, and some both for use and adornation.
GERVASE MARKHAM,
The English Hus-wife, 1615

It is now August: the Melowne and the Cucumber is now in request: and Oyle and vinegar give attendance on the Sallet hearbes. NICHOLAS BRETON,
The Boke of Moneths, 1626

Of great use in the Kitchin, and very pleasing and wholesome at the Table, is the Lettuce, an excellent Supper Sallad, cooling and refreshing.
JOHN WOOLRIDGE,
The Art of Gardening, 1688

Oh, green and glorious! Oh, Herbaceous treat! 'Twould tempt the dying anchorite to eat: Back to the world he'd turn his fleeting soul, And plunge his fingers in the salad-bowl! REV. SYDNEY SMITH,
The Lady's Annual Register, 1839

What is more refreshing than salads when your appetite seems to have deserted you, or even after a capacious dinner—the nice, fresh, green and crisp salad, full of life and health, which seems to invigorate the palate and dispose the masticating powers to a much longer duration. ALEXIS SOYER,
A Shilling Cookery for the People, 1854

The cooling sanity of lettuce and every other herbal green, whose touch is calm, whose heart is clean. LOUIS UNTERMEYER,
Food and Drink, 1952

9

Salads for Health

*I*F I stress nothing else in this my book, I want to point out the importance of raw green leaves as food. Seek them and use them above all things. They are the food Nature provides in abundance for our well-being. And salads need not be solely summer food. They can stretch through fall and winter—with cabbage, beets, carrots, and apples—till spring comes with dandelion, sorrel, lamb's quarters and the earliest of lettuce leaves. To everything there is a season? To salads every time is their season.

Salads are the liveliest vegetables we eat. The chlorophyll in green things gives the body the greatest vitality and relays the sun's forces directly to the inner man. It is the green life-blood of the plant, the giver of strength and energy. If an apple a day keeps the doctor away, so will a salad. Both are effective deterrents to medical care.

Vegetables can be limp and lifeless and still be edible if cooked, but for a zestful and appetizing salad, the ingredients must be absolutely fresh and crisp. Weary hand-handled wilted lettuce, flabby celery, soggy tomatoes and spongy cucumbers can never make a good salad. The components should be firm and are usually fibrous: crisp enough to have to be masticated, not soft and sloppy. They should stimulate the saliva and gastric juices and start digestion in the mouth.

Salads are nothing new as food, for greens were certainly foraged for in the most ancient times, and they are mentioned much in olden books I have read on food.

> Lettuce ever was, and still continues the principal Foundation of the universal Tribe of Sallets. So highly valu'd by the great Augustus, that attributing his Recovery of a dangerous Sickness to them, 'tis reported he erected a Statue and built an Altar to this noble Plant. JOHN EVELYN,
> *Acetaria,* 1699

> Lettuce and cress have, from the earliest times, occupied a most prominent place among the dinner salads. We are told that the Hebrews ate them without dressing, simply sprinkling over them a little salt. The Greeks, however, used honey and oil, while the Romans served lettuce with hard-boiled eggs, oil and spice, making a salad much more to the liking of the present generation. These salads were served as the first course. They were considered a great luxury and probably appetizers, as in those days foods were heavy and were served in enormous quantities. SARAH TYSON RORER,
> *New Salads,* 1897

Scott and I consider the eating of raw greens the most important part of our diet. Our suppers are incomplete without a salad. Instead of ending with a small salad when we have eaten our fill of other foods, we start with a large bowl of fresh raw greens or cut-up fruits or vegetables. We eat our fill of that, and then chink up the cracks, if any, with secondary provender. The start of the evening meal is always salad in some form.

Every day of the annual 365, unless we are fasting, we

try to keep raw greens a major part of at least one of our meals. If half of our diet could be raw, and at least a quarter of it green, we would find that ideal. We aim in that direction and can accomplish it even in our cold climate and in the wintertime by utilizing the roots and cabbages from our root cellar, and by sprouting seeds.

Seeds carry the life form of the future plant, the concentrated power that develops into the plant. The abundant source of vitality that is in sprouted seeds form one of the simplest and quickest and cheapest ways to add vitamins, minerals and protein to the diet.

Seeds of every kind are easily available and can be stored in bulk till sprouted. Peas, beans of various kinds (notably the mung, much used by the Chinese), lentils and other legumes, sunflower seeds, plus the cereal grasses such as wheat, oats, rye, alfalfa, are the favorites for sprouting. Sprouting increases the nutritional value of seeds, yielding more vitality than cooked seeds. The sprouts are better eaten raw, but can also be steamed or sautéed. Add raw sprouts to soups, blender drinks, sandwiches, yogurt, breads. They are most important in salads.

I have an easy way of sprouting seeds. I put a handful in a two-quart bowl, filling the bowl half-full of water. I cover it with a plate and keep in the kitchen overnight. In the morning I turn the bowl carefully upside down, keeping the plate on and catching the soak-water in another bowl. I feed this nourishing water to any houseplants we may have, or I add the water to any existing soup or soup stock. Then I cover the seeds with fresh water, stir about a bit and again pour off, with the bowl upside down and plate on tight, till all water is gone. I cover the bowl again (this time with no water on the seeds) and leave for half a day. I continue rinsing and pouring off and covering two or three times a day till little sprouts appear. When they are one or two inches long we eat them. They will keep for days in the refrigerator.

Salads need not be hampered by recipes. Use what is in season; use what is in the garden or meadow. "The country liver need never be without a salad if he will but use his eyes."[1] There are plenty of "Plants and Esculents we find at hand, delight ourselves to gather, and are easily prepar'd for an Extemporary Collation."[2] We can search the woods and fields for fresh green fodder, or confine ourselves to garden growth.

> If I should set down all the sorts of herbes that are usually gathered for Sallets, I should not onely speake of Garden herbes, but of many herbes that growe wilde in the fields, or else be but weedes in a Garden; for the usuall manner with many is to take the young buds and leaves of everything almost that groweth, as well in the Garden as in the Fields, and put them all together, that the taste of the one may amend the rellish of the other.
>
> JOHN PARKINSON,
> *Paradisi in Sole,* 1629

As to salad dressing, I go heavy on the oil, light on the vinegar, and usually make a gesture toward one or other herb. But—"Do not stir up your salad till the mouths are ready for it."[3]

> It is next to impossible to give absolute directions for the compounding of a salad, so far as the precise amount of each component is concerned—some exacting more oil and salt, some more vinegar and pepper than others—the acidity of vinegar withal being an extremely variable quantity.
>
> GEORGE H. ELLWANGER,
> *The Pleasures of the Table,* 1902

[1]Juliet Corson, *Family Living on $500 a Year,* 1888
[2]John Evelyn, *Acetaria,* 1699
[3]Mrs. N.K.M. Lee, *The Cook's Own Book,* 1832

Tossed into a bowl, it all makes a delicious blend, though it may be sharp, like dandelion or sorrel or radish, or bland and sweet, as lettuce, lamb's quarters or carrots. It does not take a genius to make a good salad, though "the wisest sheep never thought of culling and testing his grasses, seasoning them with thyme or tarragon, softening them with oil, exasperating them with mustard, sharpening them with vinegar, spiritualizing them with a suspicion of onions. The lion is generous as a hero, the rat artful as a lawyer, the dove gentle as a lover, the beaver is a good engineer, the monkey is a clever actor, but none of them can make a salad."[4]

Before I come to my own simple compounds, here are some ancient recipes you might like to try.

Take Lettice, Spinnage, Endiff, Celery, and cut half an head of Garlick amongst it, and then season it well with Oyl, Vinegar and Salt. That is a brave warming Sallet, and very wholsom.

THOMAS TRYON,
The Good House-wife Made a Doctor, 1692

A very pretty salad can be made of nasturtium blossoms, buttercups, a head of lettuce, and a pint of water cresses. It is to be covered with the French dressing and eaten immediately.

M.E.W. SHERWOOD,
The Art of Entertaining, 1892

Sage, Rosemary, Thyme, Winter and Summer Savory, Mint, Penny-royal, Parsley, Chervil, Onnions, Lettice, Sorrel, Beets both White and Red, Spinage, Cabadges or Colworts, Comfry, and many other gallant wholsome Herbs do make most excellent Sallads, which being mixt with Oyl or Butter, the Juice of Oranges and Salt, warm the Body, and more naturally and pleasantly exhillerate the Spirits than any sort of Wine drank in Moderation.

THOMAS TRYON,
Friendly Advice to Gentlemen Farmers, 1684

[4]M.E.W. Sherwood, *The Art of Entertaining,* 1892

The ultimate in appreciation of salads I found in an enconium, dateless, authorless, and titleless, though undoubtedly inspired:

A bowl of lettuce is the Venus of the dinner table. It rises upon the sight, cool, moist and beautiful, like that very imprudent lady coming out of the sea, sir. And to complete the image, sir, neither should be dressed too much.

Anyone who can put a big salad on the table can always feed a crowd adequately and wholesomely. Salads are essential to my good life.

A housekeeper who has conquered the salad question can always add to the plainest dinner a desirable dish. She can feed the hungry, and she can stimulate the most jaded fancy of the overfastidious gourmet by these delicate and consummate luxuries. To learn to make a salad is the most important of qualifications for one who would master the art of entertaining.

M.E.W. SHERWOOD,
The Art of Entertaining, 1892

BASIC SUPPER SALAD

1 head lettuce, coarsely chopped
4 tomatoes, chopped
1 green pepper, chopped
1 onion, chopped
1 unpeeled cucumber, sliced
6 spinach leaves
¼ cup chopped parsley
¼ cup oil
2 tablespoons vinegar

Combine the lettuce, tomatoes, green pepper, onion and the cucumber. Thoroughly wash and dry the spinach leaves, and tear into bite-sized pieces; add to the salad along with the parsley. Just before serving, add the oil and vinegar, tossing to coat the vegetables well. Serve immediately or spinach leaves will get soggy. Serves 6.

WINTER SUPPER SALAD

½   head lettuce or cabbage, finely chopped
    Outer stalks of 1 bunch celery, chopped
1   green pepper, chopped
3   apples, chopped
¼   cup chopped nuts
¼   cup oil
2   tablespoons vinegar

Combine the lettuce or cabbage with the celery, green pepper, apples and nuts. Add the oil and vinegar, tossing to coat the ingredients well.

SUPER SALAD FOR A CROWD

Even if people ask for seconds (which they will), this salad goes a long way! Serve it in one or more huge bowls —or even a big kettle.

1   bunch each romaine, endive and chicory
1   dandelion plant, finely cut up
1   head of cauliflower, flowerets only
3   stalks broccoli, flowerets only

1   bunch celery, chopped (including the leaves)
2   green peppers, chopped
10 small red radishes, whole
1   onion, sliced
1   carrot, finely sliced
1   cup mung bean sprouts
1   cup olive oil
½   cup cider vinegar

Thoroughly wash and dry the romaine, endive and chicory; tear into bite-sized pieces and place in a large bowl. Add the remaining vegetables, mixing well. Just before serving, add the oil and vinegar, tossing to thoroughly coat the vegetables. Serve immediately. Serves 8 to 10.

SUMMER SALAD

2   cups fresh green peas, uncooked
2   green peppers, chopped
2   carrots, slivered
2   young cucumbers, thinly sliced
½   cup minced parsley
2   tablespoons olive oil
1   tablespoon lemon juice
    Lettuce leaves

Place the peas, green pepper, carrots, cucumbers and parsley in a bowl. Toss well with the olive oil and lemon juice until the vegetables are well coated. Serve on a bed of lettuce leaves.

WINTER CABBAGE SALAD

1	small head red or white cabbage, chopped
5	apples, chopped (peel apples if skins are tough)
½	cup raisins
2	tablespoons cider vinegar
3	tablespoons olive oil

Combine the cabbage with the apples and raisins. Add the vinegar and oil, tossing to coat the ingredients well.

SPANISH SLAW

4	cups shredded cabbage
2	tablespoons olive oil
½	cup pitted black olives
1	green pepper, chopped
1	onion, chopped
1	pimiento, chopped
1	tablespoon vinegar, or to taste

Combine the cabbage, olive oil, olives, green pepper, onion and the pimiento. Add vinegar to taste and mix again.

CABBAGE MEDLEY SALAD

1	small head cabbage, finely chopped
2	apples, chopped
1	orange, peeled and cut in chunks
½	cup raisins

½ cup chopped pitted dates
1 cup chopped nuts
2 tablespoons olive oil
1 tablespoon lemon juice

Combine the cabbage, apples, orange and raisins. Stir in the dates and the nuts. Add the olive oil and lemon juice, tossing to coat the ingredients well.

CRUNCHY PINEAPPLE SLAW

1 small head cabbage, finely sliced
1 apple, diced
1 can (15 ounces) crushed pineapple, with juice
2 tablespoons olive oil
2 teaspoons lemon juice
¼ cup shelled peanuts (optional)

Combine the cabbage, apple and pineapple with its juice. Add the olive oil and lemon juice, and mix well. Just before serving toss in the optional peanuts if desired.

APPLE SLAW

3 apples, grated
½ head red cabbage, grated
2 cups celery, chopped coarsely (including the leaves)
¼ cup raisins
1 tablespoon honey
1 tablespoon lemon juice
2 tablespoons oil
Lettuce leaves

Combine the apples, cabbage, celery and raisins. Add the honey, lemon juice and oil, tossing well after each addition to coat the ingredients well. Serve on a bed of lettuce leaves.

WALDORF SALAD

4	apples, diced
2	cups chopped celery
¼	cup raisins
¼	cup chopped nuts
¼	cup oil
2	tablespoons lemon juice

Combine the apples, celery, raisins and nuts. Add the oil and lemon juice, tossing to coat the ingredients well.

Variation: If you're accustomed to using mayonnaise in a Waldorf Salad, substitute a dab of sour cream or cottage cheese for the oil and lemon juice. Either one will give the salad a creamy consistency.

QUICK BEET SALAD

4	cooked beets, peeled and diced
2	cups sliced celery
2	onions, sliced
3	tablespoons olive oil
1	tablespoon cider vinegar

Combine the beets, celery and onions. Add the olive oil and vinegar, tossing to coat the vegetables well. If not serving right away, refrigerate; this salad will keep well for several hours.

BEET SALAD

4   raw beets, peeled and grated
4   stalks celery, sliced
1   onion, chopped
2   tablespoons oil
1   tablespoon vinegar
½   cup sour cream

Mix the beets, celery and onion together. Add the oil and vinegar, tossing to coat the vegetables well. Top each serving with a blob of sour cream.

BEET & APPLE SALAD I

2   raw beets, peeled and grated
2   apples, chopped
1   cup chopped celery
1   cup raisins
1   tablespoon vinegar
1   tablespoon orange or lemon juice
2   tablespoons oil

Mix the beets, apples and celery together; add the raisins. Add the vinegar, orange or lemon juice and oil, tossing to coat the ingredients thoroughly.

138

BEET & APPLE SALAD II

4 raw beets, peeled and grated
4 apples, grated
¼ cup olive oil
2 teaspoons honey
4 teaspoons lemon juice

Place the beets and apples in a bowl. Add the olive oil, honey and lemon juice, tossing well after each addition to coat the apples and beets thoroughly.

CAULIFLOWER SALAD

1 head cauliflower, broken into flowerets
1 green pepper, chopped
6 stalks celery, chopped (including the leaves)
1 cup chopped nuts OR ½ cup pitted black olives
2 tablespoons olive oil
1 tablespoon lemon juice
   Lettuce leaves

Combine the cauliflower, green pepper and celery; stir in the nuts or the olives. Add the olive oil and lemon juice, tossing to coat the vegetables well. Serve on a bed of lettuce leaves.

GRATED CARROT SALAD

4 cups grated carrots
2 tablespoons aniseed

Juice of 2 lemons
½ cup peanut oil
2 tablespoons cider vinegar
½ cup cottage cheese

Combine the carrots with the aniseed. Add the lemon juice, peanut oil and vinegar, tossing to coat the carrots well. Serve with a dab of cottage cheese over each serving.

Variations: 1. Omit the aniseed and add ¼ cup raisins and 1 can (8 ounces) of drained crushed pineapple. 2. Add two diced apples.

MALAYSIAN SALAD

2 young unpeeled cucumbers, thinly sliced
4 stalks celery, thinly sliced
1 can (15 ounces) pineapple chunks, drained well
½ pint sour cream
½ teaspoon dill seed

Combine all the ingredients, tossing gently. If not serving right away, place in the refrigerator.

NO-LETTUCE SALAD

4 tomatoes, chopped
1 onion, finely chopped
2 cucumbers, peeled and sliced
1 green pepper, sliced

6 stalks celery, sliced
1 tablespoon cider vinegar
3 tablespoons olive oil

Combine the tomatoes, onion, cucumbers, green pepper and celery. Add the vinegar and olive oil, tossing to coat the vegetables well. This salad will keep in the refrigerator if made in advance.

GREEK SALAD

2 cups dried beans, soaked overnight in ample water to cover
2 tablespoons olive oil
2 tablespoons cider vinegar
1 small onion, minced
1 clove garlic, minced
1 cup chopped parsley
    Pinch of sea salt
    Finely chopped dandelion greens for garnish
6 black olives, quartered

Cook the beans in the water until tender—up to 2 hours. Drain off the excess liquid and save for soup, if desired. Let the beans cool to room temperature. Add the oil, vinegar, onion, garlic, parsley and sea salt, mixing until thoroughly combined. Garnish the salad with the chopped dandelion greens and black olives. Serves 6.

COTTAGE CHEESE SALAD

2 cups cottage cheese
2 green peppers, chopped
4 stalks celery, sliced
1 onion, chopped
10 pitted black olives, chopped
Lettuce leaves

Combine the cottage cheese with the chopped vegetables. To serve, mound the mixture over a bed of lettuce leaves.

ONE-INGREDIENT SALADS

Celeriac: Peel and grate a raw celery root into a bowl; add lemon juice and olive oil to taste. Or cook the celery root, cut it into cubes, and serve cold with lemon juice and oil.

Greenleaf: Plain greenleaf salads can be made by cutting up any of the following, and dressing with oil and vinegar to taste: cos, butterhead, oakleaf, iceberg, curly endive, escarole, chicory.

Radish: Scrub and thinly slice 4 dozen radishes; toss with 4 teaspoons of olive oil and 2 teaspoons of lemon juice. Serve on a bed of romaine lettuce leaves.

Belgian endive: Carefully wash 3 Belgian endives, separating their compact shape as little as possible; shake dry. Cut crosswise into 1" circles, and toss with 2 tablespoons oil and 1 tablespoon of lemon juice.

DANDELION SALAD

2 cups dried lima beans, soaked overnight in water to cover by more than 1″
6 green dandelion plants, chopped fine
¼ cup olive oil
2 tablespoons vinegar
2 tomatoes, cut in wedges

Cook the beans in the water until tender—about 2 hours. Drain off the excess liquid and save for soup, if desired. Let the beans cool to room temperature. Cut the roots off the dandelion plants, and clean the leaves carefully. Stir into the beans. Add the oil and vinegar, tossing to coat the beans well. Add the tomato wedges and stir again. Serves 6.

CHICORY BITTERSWEET SALAD

6 oranges, peeled and sliced
2 Spanish onions, chopped
1 cup chopped pitted black olives
4 teaspoons olive oil
Pinch of ground coriander
Chicory leaves

Combine the oranges, onions and olives. Add the olive oil and coriander, tossing to coat ingredients well. Tear up several chicory leaves, and arrange them on individual plates; pile the salad on top.

CUCUMBER SALAD

4 small unpeeled cucumbers, thinly sliced
6 young red radishes, thinly sliced
   Bunch of green onions, chopped
1 teaspoon fresh dill seed
1 teaspoon fresh chopped thyme
1 cup sour cream

Combine the cucumbers, radishes, green onions, dill seed and thyme. Serve the mixture dressed with the sour cream.

DRESSY WINTER SALAD

4 apples, diced
4 stalks celery, sliced
1 carrot, coarsely grated
2 very ripe bananas, sliced
1 teaspoon finely chopped fresh ginger
   Juice of 1 lemon
2 tablespoons olive oil
   Lettuce leaves
½ cup cottage cheese

Combine the apples, celery, carrot, bananas and ginger. Add the lemon juice and olive oil, tossing to coat the ingredients well. To serve, mound the salad on lettuce leaves, and top with dabs of cottage cheese.

POTATO SALAD

6   medium potatoes
1   onion, finely chopped
½   cup chopped parsley
¼   cup oil
2   tablespoons vinegar
    Pinch of sea salt

Place the potatoes in a large saucepan with enough cold water to cover. Bring to a boil and cook just until fork-tender; do not overcook. Drain the potatoes; remove the peel and slice them while they are still warm. Add the onion and parsley, and stir gently, being careful not to crush the potato slices. Add the oil, vinegar, and sea salt, and toss well to coat the potatoes thoroughly. Serves 4 to 6.

RAW POTATO SALAD

2   unpeeled raw potatoes, shredded
2   onions, chopped
1   bunch parsley, chopped
2   tablespoons olive oil
1   ripe avocado, peeled and mashed
1   teaspoon vinegar

Combine the potatoes, onion and parsley. Add the olive oil, avocado and vinegar, mixing until the ingredients are well combined. Serve on lettuce leaves.

RAW BEAN SALAD

2 cups uncooked finely sliced green beans
1 carrot, thinly sliced
½ cup raw cauliflower buds
1 small onion, sliced
¼ cup oil
2 tablespoons lemon juice

Combine the green beans, carrots, cauliflower and onion. Add the oil and lemon juice, tossing to coat the ingredients well.

ZUCCHINI-WATERCRESS SALAD

2 uncooked young zucchini, thinly sliced
3 tomatoes, chopped
1 onion, sliced, or ¼ cup chopped shallots
1 green pepper, seeded and sliced into rings
3 tablespoons olive oil
1 tablespoon cider vinegar or lemon juice
  Pinch of celery salt
  Watercress

Combine the zucchini with the tomatoes, onion and green pepper. Add the olive oil, vinegar or lemon juice, and the celery salt, stirring to coat the vegetables well. Serve the salad mounded on a bed of watercress.

SPINACH SALAD

1 pound fresh spinach
3 tablespoons olive oil
1 tablespoon vinegar
  Dash of soy sauce
½ cup mung bean sprouts
½ cup fresh green peas

Thoroughly wash and dry the spinach; tear the leaves into bite-sized pieces and place in a bowl. Just before serving, add the oil, vinegar and soy sauce, tossing to coat the spinach well. Do not do this too soon or the leaves will become soggy. Transfer the spinach to individual bowls, and garnish each serving with the bean sprouts and peas.

BEAN SPROUT SALAD

4 cups mung bean sprouts
1 cup chopped celery
4 tomatoes, chopped
1 cup minced green onion
2 tablespoons oil
1 tablespoon vinegar

Place the bean sprouts, celery, tomatoes and green onion in a bowl. Add the oil and vinegar, tossing to coat the vegetables well.

*T*HERE are many sorts of Pot-Herbs well known unto all, yet few or none doe use all sorts, but as every one liketh; some use those that others refuse, and some esteem those not to be wholesome and of a good rellish, which others make no scruple of. JOHN PARKINSON,
Paradisi in Sole, 1629

This kind of Food is preferrable to the great Quantities of Flesh, Butter, Cheese etc. which are too much eaten among us. THOMAS TRYON,
The Way to Health, Long Life & Happiness 1683

The use of Plants is all our Life long of that universal Importance and Concern, that we can neither live nor subsist in any Plenty with Decency, or Conveniency or be said to live indeed at all without them: whatsoever Food is necessary to sustain us, whatsoever contributes to delight and refresh us, are supply'd and brought forth out of that plentiful and abundant store: and ah, how much more innocent, sweet and healthful is a Table cover'd with these, than with all the reeking Flesh of butcher'd and slaughter'd Animals!
JOHN RAY, *Historia Plantarum,* 1686

If you are hungry, can't you be content with the wholesome roots of the earth?
RICHARD SHERIDAN, *The Duenna,* 1794

Here spread your gardens wide; and let the cool, the moist relaxing vegetable store prevail in each repast. DR. JOHN ARMSTRONG,
The Art of Preserving Health, 1804

It is to be regretted that the labouring poor of this country do not partake of more vegetables than they do at present. ALEXIS SOYER,
A Shilling Cookery, 1854

There is in fresh green stuff a vitalizing power, as any farmer can see when he turns his cows and colts out to grass, or supplies green stuff to growing pigs or laying hens. BERNARR MACFADDEN,
Physical Culture Cook Book, 1924

I can't quite believe the man who says he doesn't like vegetables. I simply can't see how such a wide variety of tastes, textures, and sensations can be lumped together as something to dislike. EUELL and JOE GIBBONS,
Feast on a Diabetic Diet, 1969

148

10

Vegetables for Vigor

*N*o one could mistake this little book for a complete guide
to cooking, but it may be necessary to say that it does not
even set out to be a complete guide to vegetable cooking; it tries
simply to show how to get the most nourishment and relish out
of some vegetables, and to do this without waste.

ALFRED W. YEO,
The Penny Guide, 1937

Vegetables form the main part of Scott's and my diet,
with the green leafy vegetables more predominant than
the root crops. The greener the better is our rule for
leafy crops. We prefer the outer leaves of lettuce, cabbage and celery rather than the bleached white inner
hearts, as they are richer in vitamin content. Kale, spinach, turnip and beet tops, and peas (all green) rank high
as sources of vitamin A. It is chlorophyll we're after: the
sun power or radiant energy which colors the leaves
green and thereby gives vitality and strength to the
plants and to the people who eat the greens.

149

To my amazement, Thoreau, in relating the simplicity and economy of his diet while at Walden Pond, mentions only starches. "My food alone cost me in money about twenty-seven cents a week. It was, for nearly two years, rye and Indian meal without yeast, potatoes, rice, a very little salt-pork, molasses, and salt; and my drink, water." Where were his greens; where were his vitamins and chlorophyll? He only lived for forty-five years. I am sure that more keen observations would have come down to us from his pen if he had eaten greens in abundance and therefore lived long and healthfully.

Green vegetables are the protective foods, supplying minerals, roughage and vitamins. Raw greens are a better source of vitamin C than citrus fruit. Root vegetables, cereals and starches as well as some fruits, provide the fuel and energy, the sugar and carbohydrates. Dairy products and meats provide the proteins or tissue-building for our bodies, along with dried legumes (soy beans notably) and some fruits.

> As regards the selection of vegetables, the eye can soon detect the glowing freshness which nature deposits upon such delicate articles of food as peas, asparagus, cucumbers, beans, spinach, salads of all kinds.　　　　　　　　　　ALEXIS SOYER,
> Cookery for the People, 1855

Greens are the real staff of life, not starchy bread. Vegetation is the universal food, providing us directly or indirectly with all the food we eat. Greens grow everywhere and can be eaten from the wilds as well as from cultivated gardens. "Why should you want?" asks Timon of Athens of the thieves, in Shakespeare's play of that name. "Behold, the earth hath roots; within this mile break forth a hundred springs. The oaks bear mast acorns; the briers scarlet hips. The bounteous housewife, Nature, on each bush lays her fullness before. Want! Why want?" The thieves reply: "We cannot live on grass, on berries, water, as beasts and birds and fishes."

> Man's unenthusiastic attitude to vegetables persisted almost until modern times. Few vegetables were eaten in the middle ages and even those few reluctantly. . . . Vegetables, salads and fruits were never regarded as substantial and legitimate parts of the meal. They did not come into daily use until the eighteenth century. MARK GRAUBARD,
> *Man's Food, Its Rhyme or Reason,* 1943

Vegetables are now acknowledged to be very important in the human diet. Studies in nutrition have shown that the roots, leaves and fruit of many wild and cultivated plants yield high nourishment in their minerals and vitamins. Most Americans now eat at least some vegetables daily, cooked or uncooked.

Vegetables are worthy food in proportion to their freshness and vitality when eaten. They lose some degree of their merits in proportion to the distance from market to kitchen to dinner plate. And all vegetables can only yield what nourishment they have absorbed from the soil. The garden or field of their growth should have the nutrients the plant needs and can use.

> The quality of vegetables depends much both on the soil in which they are grown, and on the degree of care bestowed upon their culture; but if produced in ever so great perfection, their excellence will be entirely destroyed if they be badly cooked.
> ELIZA ACTON,
> *Modern Cookery for Private Families,* 1845

Up to modern times vegetables were badly handled by cooks, receiving scant attention, little care or imagination. They were boiled to a pulp, and served sodden. In 1903 a lady wrote: "In England the vegetable is maltreated; in Germany it is appreciated; in France it is idealised."[1] The French are known to treat their vegetables with high respect, heightened by their cunning practice of dressing them with only the best butter.

Food values are inevitably lost in cooking, so we should learn how to cook the least and save the most. A successful cook must know what to do and how to do it. There are various ways to cook vegetables: (1)by boiling (immersing vegetables in sufficient boiling water to almost cover and cooking till tender); (2)by steaming (putting vegetables on a rack in a covered kettle, with a minimum of boiling water); (3)by blanching (plunging vegetables into boiling water, cooking for a few minutes, then draining); (4)by baking (cooking by high, continued and dry heat in an oven); (5)parboiling (blanching before baking, to cut cooking time); (6)sautéeing (slow frying with oil or butter); (7)broiling or grilling (cooking by direct contact with the fire); (8)en casserole (cooking in juices in a covered baking dish inside the oven).

Basically simple but necessary techniques for preparing and cooking vegetables include: (1)cleaning and washing; (2)peeling, chopping, slicing, dicing, grating, or leaving whole; (3)the choice of adding cold or boiling water, and how much; (4)cooking at what temperature and for how long. Let's handle these questions point by point.

(1)*First comes the raw product: cleansing and washing.* I spread out old newspapers on the sink or table

[1]Mrs. Alfred Praga, *Cookery and Housekeeping,* 1903

before I even tackle my cleaning and cutting. All the dirt and leavings can then be easily rolled up when finished and the contents thrown in the garbage pail or on the compost pile. It is a good ecological use for the tons of printed matter that flood our mailbox, and the kitchen sink and drains are left clean.

Wash leafy greens in running water if possible. Never soak vegetables in water for any great length of time. Shake the leaves and put them immediately in a sieve or the cooking kettle. Scrub carrots or potatoes under water, with the hand or a coarse brush. If cleaning beets, be careful not to break the skins in washing off the dirt, as they will bleed while cooking and lose their color. Celery and chard stalks should be carefully cleansed of earth at the base of the stems. Asparagus should be rubbed down under running water and new ends cut. Leeks need careful examination and thorough washing, for they gather dirt as they push up through the soil, and can be gritty indeed if not slit and cleaned meticulously.

(2)*Then the preparation for cooking.* Peel only when necessary. Many vitamins lie directly under the skin. Cook whole where possible. Thinly cut vegetables cook faster and more evenly than large chunks. Cube, dice or grate at the last minute to save loss of enzymes.

Quite young runner beans need no cutting; slice older ones lengthwise and take off strings. Peel the outer skins of leeks and onions; to slice them without watering the eyes, hold them when slicing under cold or running water.   ALFRED W. YEO,
The Penny Guide, 1937

(3)*How much water should be added: hot or cold?* Vegetables should not be drowned in water. There are few foods more distasteful to eat than soggy, watery vegetables that have been boiled too long and in too much water. No better way could be found to lose the water-soluble vitamins and minerals, nor a better way of losing otherwise enthusiastic vegetable-eaters.

> The practice of boiling vegetables in large quantities of water, which is afterwards poured away, is extremely absurd and injudicious; for together with the water the best and most nutritious parts of them are also thrown away.   DR. JOHN ARMSTRONG,
> *The Young Woman's Guide*
> *to Virtue, Economy & Happiness*, 1817

> Not only do vegetables have enough water to cook themselves; most of them also have enough salt. Approached in the true contemplative spirit—given a chance to speak for themselves— they are self-sufficient. There is no reason for the oceans of brine in which we usually drown them.
> FATHER ROBERT FARRAR CAPON,
> *The Supper of the Lamb*, 1969

Cook vegetables in their own juices where possible. Some greens can be cooked in heavy pots, tightly covered, with only the water that clings to the leaves after washing: for instance, spinach, cabbage, collards, kale, beet and mustard greens, and chard and turnip tops. Use a minimum amount of unsalted boiling water for other greens, with cold water recommended to start off roots, and dried vegetables, such as lentils and beans.

There are two schools of thought on cooking with tightly covered pots and cooking uncovered. Some bring to a boil under a cover and then uncover to simmer on low heat. Some boil uncovered and then cover and simmer with a bit of butter on low heat. I do both at different times. The main idea is to just use up the water and have none left over when the vegetables are tenderized. Constantly stirring food is not recommended, as the extra air reduces the vitamins. "To be perpetually lifting covers to try if a thing is done argues sad unskillfulness."[2]

(4)*Cooked at what temperatures and for how long?* I have no pressure cooker and no experience with them. I use no high temperatures once a pot boils. After being heated through, the vegetables can cook at lower heats. Once boiling, they can then simmer. I try not to cook a vegetable until it is "done," because then it is really *done,* finished, soggy, flabby and inedible. I would say: cook until just *not* done; better underdone than overdone. Halfway through cooking I pull a piece out and taste it. It should be crisp and crunchy. For whole carrots or potatoes or beets, however, a fork should be able to penetrate to the middle.

The time occupied in cooking varies, of necessity, with the type of vegetable, its age and condition, and the fire. A general rule on my wood stove is five minutes for corn; ten minutes for peas; fifteen minutes for cabbage (quartered); twenty minutes for potatoes, carrots, turnips, beans; twenty-five minutes for broccoli, cauliflower, onions and leeks, and one hour for beets.

Causing anything to boil violently in any culinary process is very ill judged, for it not only does not expedite, even in the smallest degree, the process of cooking, but it occasions a most enormous waste of fuel; and by driving away with the steam many of the more volatile and more savoury particles of the ingredients, renders the victuals less good and less palatable.

COUNT RUMFORD,
Essays on Feeding the Poor, 1798

[2]Mrs. Eliza Warren, *My Lady-Help and What She Taught Me,* 1877

Never allow vegetables of any kind to remain soaking in the water in which they were cooked. It leaches the goodness out of them. Drain immediately after cooking, and shake for a minute or two over the fire, or let stand at the back of the stove with the cover on. Throw no liquid away; save it for soup stock or for cooking other vegetables. Vitamin C is soluble in water, so be sure to use all the liquid, because that is where the power is.

Now we come to steaming. It is supposed to be the best way in cooking of preserving the vital elements, though it takes a very hot fire and I usually cook at a lower temperature. I have a small sievelike folding contraption that can be put into a pot of boiling water, with the vegetables elevated above the water. Covered tightly, the vegetables are soon cooked to tenderness by the steam alone, not needing to be immersed in the water. Without such a steamer, one can put about a cup of water in the top of a double boiler, bring it to a boil, add whatever vegetable, let it boil until the water is gone, then put the pot on top of its lower half, which should be full of boiling water. A few minutes and the vegetable is cooked.

I bake many vegetables: potatoes, in their skins, of course. I have also tried baking beets, carrots, broccoli, corn, onions, parsnips, turnips. If they are old and tough I sometimes start them off on top of the stove with a

156

minimum of boiling, and then put them in the oven. Rice and wheat are excellent, baked in the oven.

Baking is one of the cheapest and most convenient ways of dressing a dinner in small families; and, I may say, that the oven is often the only kitchen a poor man has. ANONYMOUS, *Temperance Cook Book*, 1841

Sautéeing or stewing is simmering cut-up vegetables gently in oil or a little liquid on top of the stove. It is a convenient slow way of cooking. An old cookbook has made the fetching simile that stewing is like smiling, while boiling is like laughing, and advises to "boil simperingly." (Would pressure-cooking be screaming with laughter, and frying like giggling?)

Stir-frying is a quick and easy way to cook almost any vegetable. It bastes, or half-cooks the vegetable. Instead of becoming waterlogged, it keeps its color and flavor. A wok, a deep saucerlike metal vessel, is put over the fire. Heat a spoonful or two of oil, add onions and let them simmer gently while you cut up into bite-sized pieces any other seasonal vegetables that have already been cleaned. Put the larger-sized pieces or tougher vegetables, such as carrots or celery, in the pan first, then the less firm (cauliflower or broccoli) and finally those that need the least cooking, such as scallions. Let them heat through for a minute or two, turning them over gently with a slotted wooden spoon or chopsticks. If necessary, add a few tablespoons of water and/or a dash of soy sauce. Cover with a tight lid and simmer over a low heat for five or ten minutes, till all are tender.

There are plenty of ways of cooking vegetables. Choose whichever method pleases you at the moment. But make sure the vegetables are fresh and vital.

157

See that everything you want, ready for action, may be at hand for your Stove-work, and not be scampering about the kitchen in a whirlpool of confusion, hunting after trifles, while the Dinner is waiting to be cooked.   DR. WILLIAM KITCHINER, *The Cook's Oracle,* 1817

EARLY SPRING MEDLEY

4   tablespoons oil or butter
3   onions, sliced in rings
6   outer leaves of lettuce, chopped
2   cups peas
2   carrots, sliced
2   cups asparagus, cut in pieces
1   cup tiny new potatoes

Heat oil in heavy pot. Add vegetables. Cover and cook over slow fire, stirring occasionally. When carrots are tender, take off fire and serve.

SUMMER VEGETABLE MIX

6   small carrots, scrubbed and left whole
1   turnip, peeled and sliced
1   potato, peeled and sliced
10   small white onions, left whole
3   cups young green beans, left whole
2   tablespoons butter or oil

Put all ingredients in saucepan with cold water to cover. Bring to boil and cook 15 minutes. Drain (keeping water for soup stock). Heat butter or oil in skillet and add the vegetables. Sauté 10 minutes, stirring often. For Chinese flavor, add a dash of soy sauce before serving.

CARROTS

I rarely cook carrots. They are a good raw food, eaten in their whole form, cut in strips, shredded, or put through the juicer. If you are an enthusiast for the delicious flavor and vitamin C content of carrot juice, as we are, you will save all the pulp, which undoubtedly retains a good deal of food value. Use it for salads or nut loaves or carrot breads, or even soups. Do not throw it away, though if you do, at least add it to the compost pile.

LEMONED CARROTS

3 cups carrots, scraped
2 teaspoons honey
2 tablespoons vegetable oil
1 tablespoon raisins
   Juice of ½ lemon
   Sprinkle of nutmeg

Put scraped carrots in skillet with honey and oil. Cover and cook on medium heat for 10 minutes. Stir in the raisins; sprinkle with lemon juice and nutmeg. Serve immediately.

CARROTS LYONNAISE

2   tablespoons butter
3   cups carrots, thinly sliced
1   onion, chopped
¼   teaspoon thyme
1   tablespoon honey

Melt butter in skillet. Add other ingredients. Cover and simmer for 10 minutes, turning occasionally.

HAWAIIAN CARROTS

1   small can pineapple chunks, in juice
4   carrots, sliced
2   tablespoons butter

Drain pineapple juice. Combine carrots, juice and enough water to make 1 cup of liquid. Bring to a boil. Simmer until carrots are tender, adding a bit of water if necessary. Add pineapple chunks and butter. Reheat and serve.

GUATEMALA CARROTS

3   tablespoons oil
6   carrots, sliced
2   tablespoons lemon juice
2   tablespoons honey
¼   teaspoon powdered ginger
2   ripe bananas, sliced
½   cup raisins

Heat oil in skillet and cook carrots for 10 minutes. Add lemon juice, honey and ginger. Cook 5 minutes. Add bananas and raisins and heat through before serving.

SAUTÉED PEAS AND CARROTS

Sauté in oil or butter equal amounts of raw shelled peas and raw finely sliced carrots. Cook with a handful of chopped scallions for 10 to 15 minutes, trying for tenderness. Instead of carrots, the peas can be sautéed with raw corn kernels cut from the cob.

SLICED BEETS

Wash, peel and sliver 10 young beets. Put in hot oiled wok. Add 1 tablespoon water and 1 tablespoon lemon juice and 1 teaspoon honey. Cook, covered, 10 minutes and serve very hot.

Variation: Heat 3 tablespoons butter, ¼ cup orange marmalade and 3 tablespoons orange juice. Add beets (as above) and cook, covered, 10 minutes. Serve hot.

BABY BEETS WITH THEIR GREENS

12 baby beets with their greens
2   tablespoons butter
    Dash of cider vinegar

Cut off tops to within ½" of roots. Wash greens and put aside. Clean beets under running water but do not peel. Boil 15 minutes or until fork can pierce the beets. Slip off skins under running water. Put greens in a pot with the butter. Add beets with a dash of vinegar. Stir up together and serve when greens are wilted.

SHREDDED BEETS

6 fair-sized beets, raw, peeled and shredded
1 tablespoon butter
2 cups boiling water

Put shredded beets and butter in the boiling water and cover tightly. Cook over high heat for 10 minutes. Add more butter and some sea salt, if you like, before serving.

STEWED CUCUMBERS

Cut young, 6" cucumbers in half, or quarter 10" cucumbers. If young, they need not be peeled. Sauté with sliced onions and butter and a little wholewheat flour. Add a dash of soy sauce before serving.

GREEN TOMATOES STIR-FRIED

3 green tomatoes, sliced
3 tablespoons wholewheat flour or fine cornmeal
½ teaspoon thyme

Pinch of oregano
Pinch of curry powder
2 tablespoons oil
Handful of chopped parsley

Dip tomato slices in mixture of flour, herbs and curry. Place slices in oiled skillet and simmer over low fire till lightly browned on both sides but still firm. Garnish with parsley.

STEWED TOMATOES

8 tomatoes, quartered
6 stalks celery, chopped, leaves and all
2 onions, chopped
½ teaspoon dried basil, crumbled
2 tablespoons oil

Put all ingredients in oiled skillet and simmer over low heat for 15 minutes.

HERBED ONIONS

3 onions, sliced
4 stalks celery, chopped
3 tablespoons butter
   Handful of chopped parsley
¼ teaspoon oregano

Sauté onions and celery in buttered skillet. When transparent, add parsley and oregano. Serve very hot.

ONIONS AND PEPPERS

4 green peppers, sliced
4 onions, cut in thin rings
1 clove garlic, minced
2 tablespoons olive oil

Sauté peppers, onions and garlic in the oil. Cover skillet and simmer 15 minutes.

SPICY ONIONS

6 onions, sliced
2 tablespoons oil
½ cup honey
½ teaspoon prepared mustard
½ teaspoon allspice
½ cup raisins

Simmer onions in oiled skillet. Add all else and serve with rice.

ONION-APPLE TANADA

4 onions, quartered
4 apples, unpeeled, sliced
   Handful of raisins
   Handful of sunflower seeds
   Sea salt or soy sauce

Sauté onions in oil for 5 minutes. Add apples, raisins and sunflower seeds. Cover and simmer 15 minutes. Season with sea salt or soy sauce. Good served with barley or rice.

SCALLIONS AND BEAN SPROUTS

8   scallions, chopped
3   tablespoons butter or oil
2   cups bean sprouts
1   tablespoon soy sauce
    Handful of chopped parsley

Sauté scallions in oil for 5 minutes. Stir in bean sprouts and heat thoroughly. Add soy sauce and stir. Sprinkle with parsley and serve.

LOVELY LEEKS

They are so delicate as to flavor and consistency, the less you do to them the better. Use all the good green top possible. Wash thoroughly to get all sand and dirt out. My best method to do that is to cut off the roots and then chop the stem every three inches, taking off the first outer green leaves and searching for sand. Rinse carefully in cold water. Put in oiled skillet with a dash of hot water. Cook gently for 5 minutes. Can be sprinkled with grated cheese and kept warm in the oven till wanted.

LEEKS AND RICE

6   leeks
1   cup water
2   tablespoons oil
½   teaspoon salt
2   tablespoons rice

Trim and wash leeks carefully, slicing down the middle to eliminate all dirt. Cut in 1″ lengths. Put water, oil, salt and rice in skillet and bring to a boil. Add the leeks. Reduce heat and simmer for half an hour or until all water is absorbed. Serve with a dash of soy sauce, if desired.

BAKED ACORN OR BUTTERCUP SQUASH

1   squash for each 2 people
1   teaspoon of honey and 1 teaspoon butter for each squash half

Bake squashes whole on pie plates in hot oven. When forkable, remove from oven and cut in half; remove seeds from each half. Spoon honey and butter into each squash half. Serve hot or cold.

BRAISED ZUCCHINI

Cut scrubbed squash into 2″ chunks. Sauté a few onions in oil. Add squash, a couple of cut-up tomatoes, a handful of chopped parsley. Simmer uncovered for half an hour.

ZUCCHINI MEDLEY

2   onions, sliced
4   tablespoons olive oil
1   pound zucchini, diced (need not be peeled if young)
½   pound tomatoes, chopped
2   tablespoons parsley, chopped
1   teaspoon thyme, minced
1   garlic clove, minced

Sauté onions in half of oil. Add all else. Cook in wok for half an hour.

SQUASH CUTLETS

Cut a young squash (unpeeled) into ½" slices. Fry in butter on both sides till tender. Cover with chopped parsley or a sprinkle of marjoram.

SHREDDED TURNIPS

Grate a pound of white winter turnips. Cook for 15 minutes in a skillet with 4 tablespoons oil or butter. Sprinkle with chopped parsley before serving.

GLAZED TURNIPS

3   white turnips, peeled and *diced*
3   tablespoons butter
½   cup maple syrup

Cover turnips with boiling water. Cook 15 minutes and drain. Put with butter and syrup in a skillet. Sauté until glazed, turning occasionally.

TURNIPS AND APPLES

5   small turnips, peeled and cubed
1   cup boiling water
3   apples
1   tablespoon lemon juice
2   tablespoons honey

Simmer turnips in the boiling water while peeling and cubing apples. Simmer both together until tender. Add lemon juice and honey and serve.

PLAIN PARSNIPS

Clean 6 parsnips and cut into 2" slices. Put in oiled skillet with 3 tablespoons boiling water. Cover and simmer till fork-tender. If large and tough and old, cut the parsnips crossways into ½" slices. Tenderize in a small amount of water in a covered skillet over low fire. Then take off cover and add butter to brown the slices.

BRAISED RUTABAGAS

1   cup soup stock
1 ½   pounds rutabagas, peeled and diced

2   tablespoons butter
2   tablespoons maple syrup

Bring soup stock to boil and add the rutabagas, butter and maple syrup. Cook till liquid is absorbed (about 20 minutes). Turn rutabagas in a bit more butter and serve.

STIR-FRIED RUTABAGA

2   onions, chopped
2   tablespoons oil
1   rutabaga, peeled and diced
1   tablespoon soy sauce
    Sea salt, optional

Sauté onions in oil in wok. Add rutabaga. Cover and cook 10 minutes. Add soy sauce. Cover and simmer 10 more minutes. Add a pinch of sea salt before serving.

BEET AND DANDELION GREENS

Carefully wash an abundance of both greens. Chop them up in large pieces and place them in your largest kettle with not more than an inch of water. Bring to a boil and cook only until wilted (about 10 minutes). Serve with butter, soy sauce or cheese.

SPRINGTIME GREENS WOKKED

Any greenhouse or garden thinnings of small 6"-high edible vegetables can be stir-fried. Cook just to wilting stage in small amount of oil. Add a pinch of some dried herb, a dash of cider vinegar, stir, and cook for a minute more.

PLAIN-JANE KALE

Cut kale leaves off the tough stems; wash and chop them up. Cook, covered, in a cup of water over a slow fire. Add butter and a squirt of lemon juice when serving.

STIR-FRY KALE

Cut the leaves off the tough stems of 3 kale plants. Sauté a few garlic cloves in oil. Add cut-up kale. Cover and simmer. After 10 minutes, add 3 tablespoons water, 1 tablespoon butter and 2 tablespoons soy sauce. Cover and simmer for 5 minutes more.

ENDIVES

I think cooking endives is a crime. They are best eaten raw, in salads. But in Holland I have often had them cooked. They put them in a buttered skillet, sprinkle them with the juice of a lemon, a shake of salt, a couple of tablespoons of boiling water, and cook them over the back of the stove, covered, stirring occasionally to prevent sticking. They should be done in 15 minutes.

SWISS CHARD

Wash chard leaves. Strip the green from the stems. Pretend the long white stems are asparagus or celery and treat them so by boiling in a large kettle in an inch of lightly salted water. When tender, lift out the stems and lay on a platter; drench them with butter. Meanwhile, pack a large kettle with the wet washed leaves. Cook, covered, without added water. When wilted, fork into a bowl and add butter and a dash of lemon juice.

CELERY AND PEPPERS WOKKED

1   bunch celery
4   green peppers
1   onion
2   tablespoons oil or butter
2   tomatoes
    Handful of chopped parsley

Cut outer celery stalks into ½"-thick slices, saving the tender heart for salad. Cut peppers into long strips. Mince the onion fine. Stir-fry these vegetables in oil in a wok or skillet for 10 minutes. Add wedges of tomatoes. Cook 5 more minutes. Add parsley before serving.

CELERIAC OR CELERY ROOT

These roots are knobby and hard to clean. Scrub them hard and cut off tops and any dirty parts. Peel lightly. They're great scraped and eaten raw in salads (adding a bit of lemon juice and oil). To cook, put whole cleaned root in boiling water and cook till fork-tender. Then peel and slice or chunk it. Add a bit of butter with each serving while it's hot.

A WAY TO COOK PEAS

Wash outer leaves of a head of lettuce. Put several dampened leaves of lettuce in a heavy pan. Add 2 quarts of shelled peas and an ounce of butter (no water). Cover and cook for 15 to 20 minutes, depending on heat of fire. Serve the peas and chuck the lettuce.

Variation: Wash regular pea pods (not snow peas) and put them in covered kettle with a few spoonfuls of water —just enough to keep the peas from sticking to the bottom of the kettle. Add a few spoonfuls of butter. Simmer gently 15 minutes. Serve whole. Eat by placing pod in mouth and pulling it out between teeth so as to shell the peas, stripping the nutritional parts of the pods along with the peas. Better serve paper napkins to guests!

SNOW PEAS

4 tablespoons butter or oil
½ pound young edible pod peas (about 2″ long)
½ cup water

Melt butter in wok or frying pan. Add peas. Stir. Add boiling water. Cook briskly, uncovered, until all water is gone.

CHOP SUEY

1   tablespoon peanut oil
½   quart snow peas (edible pod)
¼   head cabbage, chopped fine
1   green pepper, sliced
1   young zucchini, unpeeled and chopped
2   cups cauliflower buds
1   teaspoon cumin seed

Heat oil in wok. Add vegetables and stir. Cover and cook 10 minutes. Add cumin and stir again. Cover and cook 10 more minutes.

STEWED EGGPLANT

2   onions, chopped
2   tomatoes, chopped
3   tablespoons vegetable oil
1   eggplant, unpeeled and sliced 1″-thick
    Handful of chopped parsley

Sauté onions and tomatoes in oil for 10 minutes. Add slices of eggplant. Cook and turn till barely soft, then cover and keep simmering till wanted. Sprinkle with chopped parsley before serving.

UNCOOKED CORN

Green corn, of course, is the most immediate of all vegetables. It should be eaten before the flow of honey has stopped on the stem it has been pulled from; before the shock of their being picked has had a chance to make them sulky or nervous or revengefully tough. ROBERT TRISTRAM COFFIN,
Mainstays of Maine, 1944

Shuck the husks from fresh corn. Split rows with a sharp knife. Pare off grain and scrape all pulp from the cobs. Serve with a pinch of sea salt and oil, or even with a dash of maple syrup.

CORN ON THE COB

Heat enough water to cover the ears of corn. When water boils, add the ears. As soon as the water returns to a boil, pull pan to back of stove (or turn off the heat) and let corn stand in water, covered for 5 to 10 minutes. Then drain and eat.

Variations: 1. Put the ears of corn into cold water to cover. Bring to a boil and immediately pour off the water, leaving the cobs on back of the stove, covered, till you are ready to serve them.

2. To bake corn, remove tassles from cobs, loosening the husks but not detaching them. Run a little cold water over the cobs. Put in hot oven for 20 to 30 minutes. Each person peels his own corn and butters it.

FRIED CORN

Cut off all kernels from fresh corncobs. Melt a couple of tablespoons of butter in a frying pan or wok. Pour in corn and cover the pan. Stir occasionally, adding a little water if kept over a high fire. Can be eaten any time within 10 to 15 minutes.

WINTER SUCCOTASH

2   cups dried lima beans
2   cups dried corn kernels
    Butter
    Sea salt

Put beans and corn in separate bowls and pour plenty of boiling water over them (they will soak up enough to double their size.) Let stand overnight. In the morning, scald again by pouring more boiling water over them. Boil beans and corn separately in ample water to cover till almost tender, then simmer together for 10 minutes. Add butter and a touch of sea salt before serving.

SUMMER SUCCOTASH

3   cups fresh corn scraped from cobs
3   cups shelled green beans or limas
3   cups boiling water
    Butter
    Sea salt

Put corn and beans together in kettle of boiling water and boil for 20 minutes. Drain, saving water for soup stock. Add butter and a shake of sea salt and serve.

CREOLE CORN CHOWDER

3   cups fresh corn scraped from cobs
2   onions, chopped
2   green peppers, sliced
4   tablespoons butter
4   tomatoes, chopped
1   teaspoon honey

Stew the corn, onions, peppers and butter for 10 minutes in skillet or wok. Add the tomatoes and honey. Heat for 10 more minutes and serve.

BROCCOLI AU NATUREL

Wash, trim and separate flowerets. Sliver tender portions of stems. Put in kettle and cover with boiling water. Boil hard for 20 minutes. When forkable, drain and add a few drops of lemon juice and a dab of butter before serving.

Variation: Split up a large head of broccoli, eliminating the tough part of the stems. Separate flowerets. Cook in an inch of boiling water for 10 minutes. Drain. Sauté 2 cloves of garlic in an oiled skillet. Add broccoli and cook over low heat for 5 minutes, shaking pan occasionally. Grated cheese can be added when serving.

SKILLET CABBAGE

2 tablespoons oil
4 cups shredded cabbage
2 cups diced celery
2 onions, sliced
2 tomatoes, chopped
1 green pepper, chopped
2 teaspoons maple syrup

Oil a large skillet. Heat. Put in all ingredients. Cover and cook, stirring occasionally, for 15 minutes.

CABBAGE À LA NORA

Chop up a fresh green cabbage. Put in covered kettle with about ½ cup cold water. Add a teaspoon of vinegar (gets rid of cooking odor). Bring to a boil. From then on let simmer till tender-crisp. Add butter on table.

CABBAGE GUMBO

Take equal quantities of young cabbage chopped fine and ripe tomatoes, also chopped. Add a shredded onion and some oil. Put all in wok or frying pan without water. Stir up, cover and stew on stove for 15 minutes.

CHINESE CABBAGE

2   tablespoons oil
1   tablespoon soy sauce
1   crinkled, Chinese cabbage, chopped fine
3   scallions, chopped
    Handful of bean sprouts

Heat wok and oil lightly. Add the soy sauce. Drop the cabbage in pan and stir-fry with scallions for 5 minutes. Add bean sprouts and stir-fry another 5 minutes. Serve immediately.

SWEET-SOUR CABBAGE

½   large green cabbage, shredded
2   tablespoons oil or butter
1   apple, peeled and chopped
1   tablespoon vinegar
1   tablespoon honey
    Dash of ground cloves

Put cabbage in stew pan and add oil or butter. Cover tightly and cook for a few minutes till cabbage is limp. Add apple, vinegar, honey and cloves. Stir up and cover. Stew on the top of the stove for half an hour. Serve hot or cold.

AMSTERDAMSCHE ROTE KOHL

3 tablespoons butter
1 head red cabbage, sliced thin
1 apple, diced
3 tablespoons vinegar
1 tablespoon honey
   Handful of raisins
¼ teaspoon allspice
2 whole cloves
   Dash of nutmeg (optional)

Heat butter in skillet and add cabbage. Cook, stirring, until cabbage wilts. Add all else and cook 15 minutes, stirring often. Sprinkle nutmeg if desired.

PLAIN CAULIFLOWER

Wash 1 head cauliflower and separate the sprigs carefully. Stew in oiled skillet for 5 minutes, stirring. Add a little water or stock if too dry and stew some more. Serve with butter and a dash of nutmeg or cover with grated cheese.

PLAIN BRUSSELS SPROUTS

Trim and clean 1 quart brussels sprouts. Turn sprouts into a wok with 3 tablespoons butter or oil and cook for 10 minutes over low fire, turning occasionally. Stir in a few drops of lemon juice just before serving.

DRESSED-UP BRUSSELS SPROUTS

1   quart brussels sprouts
2   tomatoes, chopped
1   onion, chopped
2   tablespoons butter
1   teaspoon fresh thyme, minced
2   shallots, chopped

Trim and clean sprouts. Cook in ½ cup boiling water for 10 minutes. Put in skillet with tomatoes and onion and butter. Stir for a few minutes over low fire. Add thyme and shallots, and serve.

ASPARAGUS GREEN GARDEN STYLE

Wash asparagus and cut off tough ends. Place upright in tall kettle and pour 2 inches of boiling water over the stalks. Cover and boil hard for 5 to 10 minutes, according to whether you like them crisp or softer.

ASPARAGUS CHINESE STYLE

Wash asparagus and cut off tough ends. Cut across stalks on the bias, making pieces ½" thick. Heat 1 tablespoon oil in large skillet. When hot, add the cut asparagus and stir 2 or 3 minutes. Add 2 tablespoons water. Cover and cook about 5 minutes, until asparagus turn bright green.

Variation: An unusual combination is to add an equal amount of raw green peas to the asparagus and cook together.

POT SPINACH

> Spinage is an herbe fit for Sallets and for divers other purposes for the Table. Many English that have learned it of the Dutch people, doe stew the Herbe in a pot or pipkin, without any other moisture that its owne, and after the moisture is a little pressed from it, they put butter, and a little spice into it, and make therewith a dish that many delight to eate of.
>
> JOHN PARKINSON,
> *Paradisi in Sole,* 1629

Wash spinach carefully leaf by leaf. Rinse at least once. Throw into kettle whole but de-stemmed. (Save stems to be cut up small in next soup.) Add no water. Cover and simmer 3 to 5 minutes over low fire until just wilted and still bright green. Drain, keeping any liquid for soup. Keep in saucepan, covered, on back of stove till served with some butter.

Variation: After washing, put in wok with 1 minced garlic clove, 1 tablespoon soy sauce and 2 tablespoons vegetable oil. Stir until wilted. Take off stove and sprinkle on ½ cup coarsely chopped peanuts.

YOUNG GREEN BEANS

Pick green beans when they are 3″ or *less* long. Sauté them whole for a few minutes in a little butter.

Variation: They can also be cooked whole for a few minutes in boiling water and then buttered. If of mature size (3" or more), slice diagonally and very thin. Boil heartily in a minimum of boiling water for 10 minutes. Serve with butter.

POTATO TRICKS

To keep old potatoes white while boiling, add a dash of vinegar just before taking off the stove.

Start old potatoes in cold water; new potatoes in boiling water. After boiling potatoes, drain by dumping into a sieve and keep the water for soup stock. Return potatoes to the dry pot with a lump of butter. Put the covered kettle at the back of stove till needed.

Tiny new potatoes, in their skins, or peeled, can be dipped individually in sour cream, straight from the stove, or cold.

Bake tiny new or small old potatoes till crusty and eat like nuts by hand, or roll in butter.

ROASTED POTATOES

    4 potatoes
    3 onions, chopped
    ½ cup olive oil
    1 teaspoon sea salt

Scrub and peel potatoes. Cut in cubes. Put in baking bowl with onions, oil and salt. Bake uncovered in warm oven for 2 hours, stirring occasionally until potatoes are soft and browned.

SWISS APPLE-TATER

2   apples, peeled and cubed
3   tablespoons honey
1   onion, chopped
3   tablespoons butter
6   potatoes, peeled and cubed
2   tablespoons apple cider

Boil apples and honey in 3 cups water for 5 minutes. Sauté onion in butter. Add potatoes and cider to onions and cook for half an hour. Mix together with the cooked apples. Serve piping hot.

MOCK MUSHROOMS

4   leftover, cold, baked potatoes
2   tablespoons oil
4   onions, chopped
    Handful of mung beans, sprouted
1   good shake of sea salt
    Sprinkling of brewers' yeast powder

Cube the leftover potatoes, leaving the skins on. Heat oil in skillet and add potatoes and onions. Fry till browned. Add the mung beans, salt and yeast. Stir and serve hot.

Close your eyes and imagine you are eating mushrooms.

POTATOES TYROLIENNE

Cook a potful of small unpeeled potatoes in boiling water till forkable. Drain off water and leave on back of stove till peels can be easily sloughed off. Put in bowl with butter and plenty of chopped parsley or chives.

Make a whole meal of them.

POTATOES IN GREEN SAUCE

  5 potatoes
  1 onion, minced
  1 clove garlic, minced
  3 tablespoons olive oil
1½ cups vegetable stock or water
  1 cup minced parsley

Scrub and peel potatoes and cut in thick slices. Sauté onion and garlic in oil. Add the potatoes, stock, and half the parsley. Stir. Cover and bring to boil. Simmer till potatoes are tender. Add remainder of parsley. Stir and serve.

BUTTERED NEW POTATOES

2   dozen tiny new potatoes
1   onion, chopped
2   tablespoons butter
2   tablespoons water
½   cup chopped parsley

Scrub potatoes. Do not peel. Put in covered kettle or wok with all but the parsley. Stir occasionally over moderate heat for about half an hour. Add parsley during the last 5 minutes of cooking.

KASHAED MUSHROOMS

2   cups kasha (buckwheat groats)
1   cucumber, peeled and cubed
1   red pepper, chopped
1   bunch green onions, chopped fine
2   cups coarsely sliced mushrooms

Pour enough boiling water over kasha to just cover. Stir and let stand while sautéeing in wok the cucumber, pepper, onions and mushrooms. When cucumber is wilted and peppers are soft, add kasha. Stir and cook over low flame for 5 minutes and serve.

LENTIL POTTAGE

2   cups lentils
2   onions, chopped
1   garlic clove, minced

Cover lentils with water. Bring to boil and then simmer till softened. Sauté onions and garlic in oil. Add lentils (drained); stir and serve.

Variation: To give East Indian flavor, 1 teaspoon of curry powder and 1 tablespoon lemon juice can be added at the end, or a teaspoon of chopped lovage or sage or brewers' yeast can be added instead of the curry.

TOUGH OLD DRIED BEANS

Dried beans, especially soys, take a long time to cook on the stove. One apt direction for these toughies are: Soak all night and cook all day.

It has also been suggested by a rank pessimist: Put a fragment of granite into the cooking kettle along with the beans. When it is tender, the soybeans will be done.

The time can be hastened for soys, limas, favas, and brown and white beans if they are soaked in cold water to cover until they swell. Then put them in the refrigerator, or freezer, overnight. They will still take hours of boiling to soften up. Dried beans and peas should be cooked in unsalted water. If salted too soon they never soften.

Try sautéing cooked dried beans. Salt them and eat like peanuts.

TOP-OF-THE-STOVE BAKED BEANS

2   cups dried beans, soaked overnight
2   onions, chopped
2   tablespoons molasses
1   teaspoon dry mustard
1   cup tomato paste
½   teaspoon sea salt

Drain beans of soak-water and cover with boiling water, cooking till tender. On my wood stove it might take 2 hours. Sauté onions after beans are cooked. Add all other ingredients and simmer on top of stove for an hour.

CORN AND BEANS WOKKED

3   cups shelled green lima beans
2   cups raw corn cut from cob
1   green pepper, diced
1   onion, minced
4   tablespoons butter or oil

Stir vegetables in oil over low heat till beans are tender.

BROAD BEANS (FAVAS)

1 onion, chopped
1 clove garlic, minced
1 pound green fava beans, shelled
1 teaspoon coriander seed, or 1 tablespoon green
   summer savory, chopped

Sauté onion and garlic in oil. Add beans and herb. Cook covered till tender, shaking pot occasionally and adding a little water if necessary.

QUICK LIMA BEANS

2 quarts lima beans
6 tablespoons boiling water
3 tablespoons butter

Shell limas and put them in pan of boiling water. Boil with cover on 10 to 15 minutes. Add butter and serve.

LEBANESE STEW

2 cups dried fava beans, soaked overnight in ample
   water to cover
   Juice of ½ lemon

2 cloves garlic, minced
   Sea salt

Boil beans with plenty of water till tender. Drain, saving
liquid for soup stock. Add lemon juice, garlic and a dash
of sea salt. Eat hot or cold.

A ND when she homeward came, she wolde bring Wortes and other herbes
times oft, the which she shred and sethe for hir living.

> GEOFFREY CHAUCER,
> *The Clerkes Tale,* 1387

Men lived longer in those dayes because they knew the hidden vertues of
hearbs, using great continence in their dyets and behaviours. They were
ignorant of our delicate inventions and multiplied compounds. They knew not
our daintie eates nor superfluous sauces.

> WILLIAM VAUGHAN,
> *Directions for Health,* 1600

A good Huswife will gather stores of herbs for the pot, and dry them, and
pound them, and in winter they will do good service—for pot and pye.

> GERVASE MARKHAM,
> *Farwel to Husbandry,* 1676

Sick, if not well, thou'lt Herbs desire, and it shall prove, if not thy Meat, thy
Remedy.   ABRAHAM COWLEY, *The Book of Plants,* 1700

Every belle, and every beau, the most renowned knight or the most rigid
monk, welcomed alike the cinnamon, the nutmeg, the ginger, the pepper and
the clove. All the manuscripts which remain of this period abound in praise
of the spices. The facility of our intercourse with the East now has occasioned
them to be treated with less veneration, although their loss would create a
piercing outcry.   ANONYMOUS,
> *The School for Good Living,* 1814

Be extremely cautious of seasoning high. Leave it to the Eaters to add the
piquante condiments, according to their own palate and fancy.

> DR. WILLIAM KITCHINER,
> *The Cook's Oracle,* 1817

Seasoning is in Cookery what chords are in music.
> LOUIS EUSTACHE UDE, *The French Cook Book,* 1828

One of the greatest stand-bys of French cookery is herbs. The flavour they
give is one that brings the taste of a spring morning or the freshness of the
garden onto your palate.   WILSON MIDGELEY,
> *Cookery for Men Only,* 1948

190

11

Herbs & Other Seasonings

*F*OUR flavors make up our sense of taste: sweetness, sourness, bitterness, saltiness. If they occur in nature, in unadulterated foods, that is one thing. If they are added promiscuously and plenteously to whet the appetite to extra eating, it is not so good.

Foods that need high and heavy seasoning before they are considered edible had best be left uneaten. If cooked food tastes flat and insipid without salting and peppering, there obviously is something wrong with the food or the cooking. Salt and pepper are added to bring back to life what has been killed in cooking. The natural untampered-with foods contain all the elements necessary for proper functioning of the body. No food value is added by the use of salt, pepper, mustard or spices, and much can be lost. Spices were originally used as preservatives and have come to be regarded as necessary flavorings.

The need for sharp condiments is a stigma on the cook, who cannot serve up a tasty dish without additives to apparently unpromising material. "Saucing," one nineteenth-century author claims, "is the refuge from bad cookery."[1] The competent culinary artist ought to be able to avoid excessive use of all spices and condiments, which often are used to hide defects in food. If a disguise is needed, it is poor food and should be shunned.

A Yorkshire farmer, seeing an overpainted lady from the city, remarked succinctly: "It be poor land as needs all that muckin'." I think it be poor food that needs all the condiment-muckin' that people add. Food should taste like what it is, not something else.

> Salting and spicing are to be effected with such caution that the diners may never be inconvenienced by excess.
>
> J.L.W. THUDICUM,
> *The Spirit of Cookery,* 1895

So many foods today have salty and peppery flavors added before they reach the table. Even so, people (like Scott's father) salt food heavily before tasting it. This kind of salt addiction tends "to develop the same contempt for ordinary unspiced food that the alcohol user does for weak tea. . . . The use of hot spices, of which pepper is the most common, is a habit almost as artificial as alcohol or tobacco."[2]

> This Spice [pepper] being too much eaten, wounds Nature to the very Heart. The truth is, this hot fiery Sawce does powerfully stir up and beget Appetite, and warms the Stomach, which does intice many to eat it with their common food, but they never consider the mischiefs it brings unto Health. . . . The worst of all is, after our Stomachs are acustom'd to such things, we cannot be

[1]E.S. Dallas, *Kettner's Book of the Table,* 1877
[2]Bernarr Macfadden, *Physical Culture Cook Book,* 1924

well satisfied without them, for they are in some degree like wine, whereof if a man drink frequently he cannot without a great deal of Trouble refrain from it.　　THOMAS TRYON,
Friendly Advice to Gentlemen Farmers, 1684

"Don't you think," asked Salinda, "that salt is necessary?" "No more," said Mr. Savery, "than any of the other stimulants. If we eat less salt, we should drink less, and the world would be saved from the disgrace of drunkenness. We are so accustomed to the use of salt that we never stop to inquire whether it is really useful or necessary, or beneficial, or otherwise."　　SOLON ROBINSON,
How to Live, 1860

Salt is not a food. It is an anti-biotic (against life). It is an inorganic chemical, a foreign irritant, a pickling agent —hard and sharp of itself, and unpleasant to those who are not addicted to its stringent qualities. The Indians of North America and other primitive peoples did not use salt as seasoning; they found it occurring naturally in the foods they ate. The body needs natural salts, but in organic form, as found in plant life.

Unassimilated and unabsorbed in the body, inorganic salt builds up and lodges in the joints and helps cause arthritis. It robs the body cells of their liquids and results in serious complaints ranging from high blood pressure to bloating edema. Obese people are usually salt-consumers. They are carrying gallons of water to keep the salt they eat in solution—the body's attempt to prevent salt poisoning. Drop the salt habit and eliminate the extra pounds. Go easy with the salt shaker!

In all the cookbooks I am acquainted with, a great or greater dose of salt is a fixture in every receipt; and hardly a dish or preparation is named in which a "pinch" or "teaspoonful" or "tablespoonful" of salt is not prescribed as one of the ingredients.
DR. RUSSELL THACKER TRALL,
The New Hydropathic Cook Book, 1854

> The less Salt any shall eat, the less they will covet it; for the mixing of common Salt with sundry sorts of Vegetable Foods does hide or Eclipse the fragrancy and pleasant Taste of the Essential Salt, that it cannot be felt by the Palate.
>
> THOMAS TRYON, *The Good House-wife Made a Doctor,* 1692

Salt is added to foods to restore the flavor lost in cooking. Eat raw food with the original organic salts intact and you won't need to add salt. By making your foods salty you reduce them all to the same plane and disallow the natural tastes to manifest. The taste buds are wrecked when deadened by omnipresent salt and peppering. Accustomed as we are to what Thoreau calls (in a rare, for him, pun) "that grossest of groceries," it is difficult at first to get along without it. Gulliver, in his travels in the Houhynhnm's country, said: "I was at first at a great loss for salt, but custom soon reconciled the want of it; and I am confident that the frequent use of salt among us is an effect of luxury."[3]

I have grown up in an age of addiction to salt and occasionally throw it into a soup that seems bland. When I do use salt, it is sea salt. If you are a confirmed saltperson you will use it anyway, but it is not necessary for an unpolluted palate. Season if you like and as you like, but these recipes are healthier unsalted.

There is another seasoning, as strong as salt, from the vegetable kingdom: garlic. Because of its biting taste and overpowering smell, it has been exorcised from polite society. Thomas Hyll, in 1563, urged it "to be discretely eaten." John Evelyn, in 1699, warns " 'Tis not for ladies' palats, nor those who court them.' "

---

[3]Jonathan Swift, *Gulliver's Travels,* 1727

Much more of Garlick would be used for its wholesomeness, were it not for the offensive smell it gives to the by-Standers.
JOHN WOOLRIDGE, *The Art of Gardening*, 1688

A little garlic, judiciously used, won't seriously affect your social life, and will tone up more dull dishes than any commodity discovered to date.   ALEXANDER WRIGHT,
How to Live Without a Woman, 1937

Garlic used as it should be used is the soul, the divine essence, of cookery. The cook who can employ it successfully will be found to possess the delicacy of perception, the accuracy of judgment, and the dexterity of hand which go to the formation of a great artist.   MRS. W.G. WATERS,
The Cook's Decameron, 1920

There seem to be garlic lovers and garlic haters. I use it in salads, and to brighten soups, and in dishes that might be too bland for the ordinary taste. Cooked, it loses much of its power. Raw, it is too fiery for many people. As to overcoming the smell for polite society, chewing raw parsley after consuming garlic will save you from being a social outcast.

Ginger, cardamom, nutmeg, cloves and cinnamon added to vegetables make for extra Oriental flavor. Toasted seeds and chopped nuts add variety, if you are not afraid of getting too ornate. If you have lemons or lemon juice around, squirt some on almost any vegetable just before serving, instead of, or along with, butter. Try a little lemon juice with green beans, brussels sprouts, broccoli or asparagus, or even lima beans.

The delicate nonirritating flavors of harmless garden herbs are all that are really necessary if cooked food needs extra savor. The fetish for artificial flavorings can best be allayed by using this mildest of additives—herbs —which the ancients divided into three categories: *pot herbs,* such as lettuce, chard, spinach, sorrel, whose

195

leaves were used for salads and soups; *seasoning herbs,* such as tarragon, fennel, thyme, basil, dill, sage; and *garnishing herbs,* such as parsley, scallions, watercress, chives. The seasoning herbs are those that can take the place of the fiercer flavors of spices and salt and pepper. Their ripened seeds possess an aromatic flavor that can be added to soups, sauces, salads and stews.

A caustic English writer (who does not know that I, for one, wear pants year-round), gives her idea of an herb garden as "a small and somewhat self-conscious plot used doubtfully as flavourings by vegetarian cooks in skirts of hand-woven tweed."[4] We have an herb garden (rather large, and I hope conscious of itself), and grow, or have grown, all of the following: peppermint and spearmint, borage, thyme, tarragon, rosemary, marjoram, dill, hyssop, sage, equisetum, lemon balm, lavender, comfrey, camomile, basil, bee-balm, summer and winter savory, tansy, oregano, lovage, coriander, caraway, rue, nettles, mullein, yarrow, catnip, and others I can't remember.

I make use of these herbs all year round: green in the summertime, and during the rest of the year from my store of dried or frozen herbs. "It is especially in winter that the cook should be provided with a plentiful supply of dried herbs."[5] If substituting dry for fresh herbs, far less is needed for flavoring: a pinch; whereas with fresh, a handful before chopping might be the rule. (Half a teaspoonful of dry herbs equals one tablespoon of fresh.)

> Dryed Herbs, Seeds, Grains and the like, when committed to any proper Liquor, do more freely give forth their good Virtues, than the Green. THOMAS TRYON,
> *The Way to Health, Long Life & Happiness,* 1683

[4]Nan Fairbrother, *Men and Gardens,* 1956
[5]An English Physician, *French Domestic Cookery,* 1825

Always gather herbs when in bud, before flowering or seeded. Cut off the tender last few inches of short herbs like thyme and lemon balm and marjoram or summer savory, and dry quickly on trays in a warm room or lukewarm oven. Taller herbs, like mint or basil or sage, can be cut off near the ground and hung up to dry. Then strip from their stems and store in airtight, lightproof containers and put in a cool place. Crumble in your hands when adding to food, not before. Breaking into small pieces before using causes herbs to lose flavor. If herbs are overcooked their flavor will be lost, so add to soups or other dishes only toward the end of the cooking process.

If gathering herbs for freezing, snip sprigs just before flowering, wash and shake dry and seal in plastic bags or containers and put in freezer. Dill seeds, for instance, can be cut off before ripening, while still green, and frozen for use all winter. I have also frozen fresh parsley (not so successfully) for use in winter soups.

One can make little "faggots" or bunches of varied herbs: parsley, thyme, tarragon and chervil, using them fresh in soups or juices. The American Indians collected the small twigs of chokeberry and wild cherry, tied them in little bundles with strips of bark and dropped them into their boiling kettles. There are so many growing things in field and forest to use. "Oh, we can make liquor to sweeten our lips, of pumpkins, of parsnips, of walnut-tree chips," runs an old song.

Our home tea may differ daily; sometimes it is plain mint leaves or camomile flowers from the herb garden, or clover blossoms from the meadow, or raspberry, strawberry or blueberry leaves from the berry patch. But I usually start with a dried rose hip base. The ingredients vary with the season, or with the crop, or with what is hanging drying on the kitchen timbers, or what my hand goes to in the drawer of herbs in tins.

I make a tea of a dozen or more different herbs, which I have marketed as *Dozen Herb Tea*. The contents ranged from shredded equisetum, thyme, various mints, camomile, catnip, comfrey, basil, lavender blossoms, summer savory, lemon balm, marjoram to rose hips. I have made other combinations, such as dried leaves of strawberry, blueberry, raspberry, rose petals, clover blossoms, with ground-up orange and lemon peel and cloves for added flavor, which I call *Meadowsweet Tea*. A good friend of mine, Juliette de Bairacli Levy, gathers many aromatic herbs from the hills of Galilee; to this connoisseur's tea she adds powdered spices (which gave me the idea for the clove).

Delicious dips can be made of dried and chopped garlic, onion, parsley, oregano, dill and celery seed stirred into sour cream. Or this combination may be judiciously scattered into a salad or onto a steaming hot, newly opened baked potato.

Here are some of my herb kitchen-uses in cooking. They are only suggestions, as, generally, any herb is good with any vegetable, but try which combinations you prefer.

Summer Savory can be added to any soup, or to green beans. Simmer the savory with a minced garlic clove and a chopped onion in olive oil, and pour over the beans. It is good with cabbage, sauerkraut, peas, lentils, potatoes, and also green salads.

Parsley contains as much vitamin A as cod-liver oil and three times as much vitamin C as oranges, but it is used mostly just for a garnish, tossed aside on the dish and back it goes to the kitchen, to be thrown away with the garbage. We use it, dry or fresh, in nearly all soups, or chopped green in salads. It can be stirred into mayonnaise, and is good with butter on baked potatoes. We cut the stalks in the garden and hang them to dry on our kitchen timbers. I also freeze the small sprigs. When I have a great batch of parsley (Scott sometimes goes over the plants in the garden and brings a whole pailful into the kitchen) I sauté them for not more than a minute in a hot pan. While still green, before browning, I take them out and serve at once.

Parsley is the most universally used in the Kitchin of all Garden Herbs. It is an excellent Ingredient in most Pottages, Sawces, and Sallads.

JOHN WOOLRIDGE,
The Art of Gardening, 1688

Basil is traditionally used with tomatoes, either when cooked or eaten raw in salads. I always add basil to my tomato soups and juices, as well as an occasional pinch in green salads.

Hyssop is a hardy herb we grow in abundance in our herb garden. I have used it only in teas.

Hyssop is an hearbe to purge and clense raw flegmes, and hurtful humors from the Brest. The same unto the lungs great comfort lends, with hony boyl'd: but farre above the rest it gives good colour, and complexion mends, and is therefore with women in request.

SIR JOHN HARYNGTON,
The Schoole of Salerne, 1607

Marjoram is very pungent. It is good with string beans if used with discretion, also with mushrooms, lentils and with cottage cheese. To make a special vinegar, fill a glass jar with marjoram leaves. Pour vinegar into the jar to fill. Cover and leave on a sunny shelf for two weeks. Strain and use.

Lavender can be treated the same way to make a vinegar. I add lavender to teas, or combined with lemon balm and sage it makes a special tea.

Dill is usually known as a flavoring for dill pickles, but is also good in salads, green or dried, or sprinkled over boiled potatoes. Both seeds and leaves have strong flavor.

Chives come early in the season and are at their best before the bloom appears. Chop up fine for their delicate flavor in salads, soups and cottage cheese, and over cooked carrots.

Rosemary is a stringent herb. Use sparingly in soups or fruit salads. Added to rose hip tea (which is fairly tasteless) it gives a gingery flavor.

Sage is another strong-tasting herb. It is good for stuffings and soups, particularly tomato soup. Try a small amount in baked beans, or a few finely crushed leaves in cottage cheese.

Caraway seeds can be added to applesauce. Beets are good with caraway seeds sprinkled over a yogurt or sour cream dressing.

Tarragon is much used by the French, mostly to flavor vinegar. I put it judiciously into sour cream for salad dressing.

Celery leaves, green or dried, give the flavor of the plant to soups. The seed can be put in stews.

Lovage imparts a racier celery flavor and should be used sparingly in all but soups. Try rubbing a salad bowl with the crushed green leaves. It can also be cooked as a vegetable green, when fresh.

Mint is a much-used herb. Mostly put in teas, it is also pleasant in tossed salads; mixed with cottage cheese, or stirred up with vinegar and honey for a light sauce. It adds a fresh flavor to cooked peas or carrots.

All Mints are good for the Stomach, and fortify it much; they create an Appetite, revive the Heart and Brain; they resist the Malignity of Poison, kill the Worms, help Women's Terms and hard Labour, are of a dissolving and detersive Nature.

DR. M.L. LEMERY,
A Treatise of All Sorts of Foods, 1745

Comfrey leaves, when young, can be cooked, or eaten in salad. We dry the leaves and add them to our herb teas.

Thyme is one of my favorites. It goes mainly into soups and stir-fried dishes.

Fenugreek is grown for its seeds. With lemon juice and honey it makes a good tea.

The Herb Fenugreek with Pickles, Oyl and Wine was a Roman Dainty. It is plainly a Physical Dyet that will give a Stool, and mix'd with Oats, it's the best Purge for Horses. An excellent Invention for Frugality, that nothing might be lost, for what the Lord did not eat he might send to his Stable. WILLIAM KING, *The Art of Cookery,* 1709

Final advice on the judicious and optional use of flavorings is in a story Scott has told me of a woman he knew in the 1890s, the wife of a judge in Blossberg, Pennsylvania. Mrs. O.F. Taylor was an exceptionally good cook and was often asked for recipes after folk had sampled her excellent meals. She would obligingly write them out in delicate longhand, invariably adding at the end of her detailed description of how she made her dishes: "And season with a little gumption."

Now set for thy pot Best herbs to be got. For flowers go set All sorts ye can get. THOMAS TUSSER, *Five Hundreth Pointes of Good Husbandrie,* 1557

*T*HE true economy of housekeeping is simply the art of gathering of all the fragments, so that nothing be lost. . . . Nothing should be thrown away so long as it is possible to make any use of it, however trifling that use may be.　　　　　　　　　　　　　　　　　　LYDIA MARIA CHILD,
The American Frugal Housewife, 1829

This Book is a Save-all. It suffers nothing to be lost.
SIR THEODORE MAYERNE,
Excellent & Approved Receipts & Experiments in Cookery, 1658

One important art in housekeeping is to make what remains from one's day's entertainment contribute to the elegance or plenty of next day's dinner.
JOHN TIMBS,
One Thousand Domestic Hints, 1871

There is enough nutriment, in the form of so-called scraps, flung daily into the dustbins and streets of New York to provision a man-of-war for a three years' cruise.　　　　　　　　　　　　　　　　　　　　　R. TOMES,
The Bazar Book of the Household, 1875

The housekeeper who is ingenious, who enjoys trying experiments with her cooking, and who has intelligence and enthusiasm combined, may find out many ways for herself of using left-over pieces, that will be better than anything she may learn from the cook-books.　　　　SALLIE JOY WHITE,
Housekeepers and Home-Makers, 1888

Admirable flavorings are given by the little leftovers of vegetables that too often find their way into the garbage bucket.　　　SARAH TYSON RORER,
Left Overs, 1898

Some of the finest cooking in the world is based on leftovers.
MARIE A. ESSIPOFF, *Making the Most of Your Food Freezer*, 1951

A man once said his wife had a wonderful way with leftovers—she threw them out. Poor man and poor wife! Some of the most succulent dishes I've eaten have been made with leftovers, to say nothing of the dollars saved by using them.　　　　　　　　　　　　　　　　　　BEATRICE VAUGHAN,
The Old Cook's Almanac, 1966

12

Leftovers & Casseroles

*I*F I were a Rockefeller and had plenty of money, I know I would still be economical—turn off lights, save string, paper bags and wrapping paper, and not throw away good food just because there is plenty more in the larder. There are few leftovers that cannot be used in other dishes if made up promptly and combined with discrimination.

We have friends with less income than we and who live far richer and more extravagantly as regards food. They throw away what I would make meals of; they do not keep a stockpot; they buy needlessly from the stores; they set a more varied table; they eat what I would call an affluent diet. I know few Americans who feed simpler or easier or cheaper than we do.

Save everything, even if it is only a tablespoon of stewed tomatoes or one of peas; they may be added to tomorrow's omelet and change it from a plain into a dainty one. If the yolk of the egg has been used for a sauce, save the white, and in arranging for the next day's dinner select a dessert in which it may play a part. If there is one cold boiled potato, save it; you may have cream of potato soup without the cooking of an extra potato. A few ears of corn may be cut off and added to breakfast muffins, or to the omelet, making corn muffins and a corn omelet. A pint of stewed tomatoes will make a tomato sauce for croquettes.

SARAH TYSON RORER, *My Best 250 Recipes,* 1907

This lady certainly made the most of scraps. She does not, however, mention the nutrients that would otherwise be lost. It is well-known that water in which vegetables have been boiled abounds in nourishment and can always be added to soups. The water that dried beans or peas or wheat seeds have soaked in overnight can also be utilized, if only to water your houseplants.

"Gather up the fragments that remain, that nothing be lost," says John, in his Sixth Gospel in the Bible. Casseroles can use leftover food. Such one-dish meals can be economical of material and of time, being put together in a matter of minutes. They need not be a mishmash of garbage, incongruous food mixtures, into which "anything goes." "We loathe to see mixtures where gentlefolk dine, which scarcely look fit for the poultry and swine."[1]

One scornful and extravagant chef, when asked what to do with leftovers, replied: "Buy a Great Dane." Acknowledgedly, in professional kitchens much must be thrown away because preparation for the next meal presses, and time cannot be taken off juggling with bits of this or that. But home cooks, with half a mind and half a minute, can use much that might otherwise go down the drain or onto the compost pile.

There is the pot-luck simplicity of stews, for in-

[1]Caroline B. Piercy, *The Shaker Cook Book,* 1953

stance, that can take carrots, turnips, potatoes, leeks, celery, peas or any sort of vegetable that is at hand, cut up small, with a bit of liquid added (oil or water or milk) and a few herbs. In Holland such a vegetable dish would be called hutspot, and in old England, Hodge Podge. There are many thrifty (not necessarily parsimonious) cooks I know who never throw away pea pods, the coarse parts or green tops of celery, or beet or turnip greens. If not wilted and aged they are chopped up and put to use.

The materials should be fresh and tasty if meager in quantity. They should not be wilted or worthless. There are those people who scrimp so much that they will not eat good quality food but sniff for bargains and use food that has gone by. To save, they pass by the perfect fruit, which will keep, and are always eating the rotten apples. It is good to live frugally but not wretchedly.

Nothing can be more distant from the thoughts of the writer of the following tract, than a wish to encourage anything like meanness or stinginess.   WILLIAM A. ALCOTT,
Ways of Living on Small Means, 1837

Frugality does not imply parsimony any more than extravagance comprehends generosity. Economy does not signify stinting of food, lack of variety, and insufficient quantity. It means judicious buying, good cooking and a consideration of left-overs so that they may appear upon the table in attractive shape.   CHRISTINE TERHUNE HERRICK,
Housekeeping Made Easy, 1888

Somebody has said that a well-to-do French family could live on what an American household in the same condition of life wastes. This may not be a great exaggeration. My mother was Dutch and a very saving woman. I learned from her to be frugal (while my extravagant high-living sister says she learned from my mother's cheese-paring to spend and waste). Speaking of paring, I can analyze a person's kitchen attitudes (and characteristics in general) by the way they peel a potato or apple. They are surely wasteful and extravagant if on cutting open an apple they cut out a large section of the core and take off great slabs of skin from apple or potato. I place them in the squandering class and keep them from helping me at the sink. If, like me, they cut and peel with a sparing hand, I deem them careful and frugal in all their dealings.

This has little to do with their class or financial background. It seems to be an inborn characteristic. One of my (and Scott's) favorite stories is of the well-to-do lady who invariably saved quantities of string. After she died they found boxes and boxes of carefully untangled and wound-up string—the accumulation of decades. One box that was full to overflowing was labeled "String Too Short to Save." I salute this lady and wonder how she is occupying her time in the hereafter: scanning heaven's floor for bits of string?

In an old Scotch cookbook I came across a recipe calling for "½ egg." That is carrying economy a little far. And anyway, what a messy job to divide this egg. And how, where and when use the other half? This cook must have been crazy or a genius.

Mary Kettilby, in 1714, in her *Collection of Above 300 Receipts,* writes of "a splendid Frugality." There need be no meanness or avarice implied in strict husbandry.

In times of prosperity and affluence there might be excuse for unthriftiness (though never for spendthriftiness). Now, in our day of the ten-cent dollar, when prices and costs are rising sky-high, we should learn how to tighten our belts and live on as little as we can, saving what we have today to help ourselves or someone else tomorrow.

> Instead of helplessly wringing our hands and crying out about the high price of fuel and food, let us accept the present state of things and brace ourselves up helpfully and bravely to face the increased cost of the necessities of life. If fuel and food cost nearly twice as much at present as they did ten years ago, then surely it becomes our imperative duty to see how we can, each of us, according to our possibilities, make the material for warmth and cooking go twice as far as they have done hitherto.   LADY BARKER,
> *First Lessons in the Principles of Cooking,* 1874

I don't make casseroles often: too much of a mixture of different things for my taste. But there are advantages in casserole cooking. The dish may be made in advance. It can be left in the oven unwatched and still tastes good if a bit overcooked. It can utilize a warm oven already in use, and it can be served in the original cooking vessel.

Here are some of my simple ways to use inexpensive ingredients and make them palatable and nutritious.

DUTCH HUTSPOT

6   potatoes, scrubbed, peeled and sliced
3   carrots, scrubbed and sliced

3 onions, sliced
½ cup fresh herbs (parsley, dill, basil) or
   1 tablespoon dried
1 tablespoon oil

Stir vegetables together and put with herbs and oil in casserole. Cook in hot oven for an hour.

POTATO CASSEROLE

6 smallish potatoes, scrubbed and sliced (need not be peeled)
6 stalks celery, sliced
6 onions, sliced
4 tablespoons butter or margarine
½ cup grated or chunked cheese

Put potatoes in a baking dish. Add the celery. Fill the dish with the onions. Add cold water to just cover and dot with pieces of butter. Bake covered in slow oven 3 hours, adding more water if necessary. Uncover for last hour, adding the grated or chunked cheese.

SCOTCH STOVIES

2 onions or leeks, sliced
6 potatoes, peeled and sliced
½ cup butter or margarine
1 cup stock or water
   Handful of chopped parsley

Arrange onions and potatoes in layers in casserole, dotting with butter. Add stock liquid. Cover and bake in a hot oven 1 hour or until potatoes are soft. Sprinkle generously with parsley and serve.

CANDIED YAMS OR SWEET POTATOES

4   yams or sweet potatoes, scrubbed but unpeeled
½   cup butter or margarine
1   cup water
4   tablespoons maple syrup
1   teaspoon ground orange peel
½   teaspoon cinnamon
½   teaspoon nutmeg

Cook sweet potatoes in boiling water or steam until tender. Then peel and slice. Meanwhile, mix together the butter, water, maple syrup, orange peel, and spices in a pan and heat till the butter melts. Put a layer of yams in a baking dish. Pour a third of the butter mixture over it. Repeat until all ingredients are used. Bake in slow oven for half an hour.

HERBY TOMATOES

1   tablespoon oil
½   teaspoon fresh basil leaves, chopped
½   teaspoon fresh marjoram, chopped
½   teaspoon fresh parsley, chopped
2   garlic cloves, minced
4   tomatoes, cut in half crossways

Mix together oil and herbs and garlic. Put tomato halves in pie plate or ovenproof dish. Spoon herb mixture onto tomato halves. Bake in slow oven 15 minutes. Tomatoes should keep shape and not get mushy.

SAVOY CABBAGE

1   large savoy cabbage, quartered
3   tablespoons butter
1   cup dried breadcrumbs

Pour boiling water over cabbage to cover, and let stand for 10 minutes. Drain well (saving juice) and put in buttered casserole. Cover with breadcrumbs browned in butter. Heat in warm oven for 10 minutes.

BAKED MUSHROOMS

1   quart mushrooms
1   cup chopped scallions
1   cup sour cream
    Dash of soy sauce

Clean mushrooms. Leave whole. Place in a baking dish along with the scallions, sour cream and soy sauce. Cover and bake in moderate oven for an hour.

BAKED EGGPLANT

1   eggplant, diced and not peeled
2   onions, sliced
2   tomatoes, chopped
1   tablespoon basil leaves or oregano
½   cup grated cheese

Layer eggplant, onions and tomatoes in baking dish. Top with sprinkle of basil leaves or oregano and the grated cheese. Bake for half an hour in moderate oven.

NO-FRY EGGPLANT

1   eggplant
    Mozzarella cheese
    Tomato sauce, 1 small can

Slice the eggplant (unpeeled) into 1″ rounds. Place as many as you can in one layer on the bottom of an oiled casserole dish. Cover with a layer of sliced mozzarella cheese. Repeat layer until all eggplant is used. Finish with the cheese, and pour over the whole lot a small can of thick tomato sauce. Bake in hot oven about an hour.

ZUCCHINI

2   onions, sliced
3   cups cubed zucchini (if young, need not be peeled)
2   tomatoes, chopped
½   cup grated cheese

Sauté onions in oiled pan. Stir in the zucchini and tomatoes. Cook for 5 minutes. Put in casserole and top with the grated cheese. Bake uncovered in moderate oven for ½ to ¾ of an hour.

COUNTRY CASSEROLE

1 clove garlic, minced
1 tablespoon oil
1 cup green beans, finely sliced
1 cup shelled peas
¼ head cabbage, sliced fine
3 leaves swiss chard, torn
   Flowerets from ½ cauliflower
4 spinach leaves, torn
¼ cup boiling water

Sauté the garlic in oil. Toss the vegetables into the pan and stir. Add a bit of boiling water and cover. Simmer till beans are chewable.

LEEK STEW

5 leeks, washed carefully and sliced into 1″ pieces
4 carrots, sliced
4 stalks celery, sliced
2 potatoes, sliced
3 tablespoons butter

Place sliced leeks in heavy casserole. Layer equally with carrots, then celery, and top with potatoes. Pour 1½

cups water over all. Add some dabs of butter. Cover and
cook slowly on top of low fire or in slow oven for about
an hour.

CASSEROLED CARROTS

1   pound carrots, grated
3   tablespoons butter or oil
3   tablespoons water
3   tablespoons maple syrup
    Dash of sea salt

Mix all in a casserole. Cover and cook in warm oven for
an hour.

VEGETABLE CASSEROLE À LA GRANDE

1   eggplant, cubed but unpeeled
2   tomatoes, sliced
1   young zucchini, chopped but unpeeled
1   green pepper, sliced
1   onion, sliced
1   cup chopped celery
1   cup shredded cabbage
4   cloves garlic, minced
2   cups chopped parsley
1   teaspoon oregano or basil
½   cup olive oil

Arrange vegetables in layers, one layer at a time. Mix
together the minced garlic, parsley and oregano, and

sprinkle mixture over each layer. Sprinkle each layer with oil. Bake uncovered 1 to 2 hours in a moderate oven.

PUMPKIN SHELL CASSEROLE

1   10- or 12-inch pumpkin or winter squash
4   apples, cubed and unpeeled
1   cup raisins
1   cup chopped nuts
2   oranges, peeled and chopped
½   cup maple syrup or honey
¼   teaspoon cinnamon
¼   teaspoon nutmeg

Scrub the pumpkin or squash, leaving the stem on for a handle. Carve out a 5- or 6-inch circle from the top and save for a cover. Dig out seeds and soft interior and discard. Mix all ingredients together and spoon them into the shell. Put on the lid and place the filled shell in a hot oven on a pie plate. Bake until a fork can easily penetrate the shell. To serve, remove the cover and serve on the table from the shell.

LIMA BEAN CASSEROLE

2   cups dried lima beans
2   cups chopped onions
1   tablespoon oil
¼   pound grated cheese

½   teaspoon sea salt
1   cup chopped nuts

Soak the dried limas in plenty of water overnight. Drain in the morning and cook the limas in fresh water (to cover amply) till tender. Simmer the onions in oil. Add the beans and stir together with the cheese. Put all ingredients in baking dish and bake for an hour in warm oven.

BAKED SOYBEANS

2   cups dried soybeans
¼   cup peanut butter
1   onion, chopped
1   cup tomato juice
    Dash of soy sauce
    Sprinkle of cumin seed or ground cardamom

Soak dried beans overnight in ample water to cover. Drain (saving water for soup stock). Bring the beans to boil in fresh water to cover, then reduce heat and simmer 2 hours. When tender, drain. Place in casserole with all other ingredients. Bake for 2 hours in warm oven. Baste, if necessary, with some of the drained bean water.

BAKED BEANS

2   cups dried beans, soaked overnight
1   onion, chopped
½   cup maple syrup or molasses

1   teaspoon dry mustard
½   teaspoon vinegar
1   teaspoon curry powder
4   tablespoons oil
1   tomato, diced

Cook beans in fresh water till skins burst. Drain, reserving liquid. Put all ingredients except tomato in baking pot. Bake, covered, 3 to 4 hours in moderate oven, or all day if you have a wood stove, adding a little bean water as pot goes dry. Uncover for last hour and add diced tomato.

FRUITY BAKED BEANS

2   cups dried beans, soaked overnight
1   onion, chopped
2   apples, diced
½   cup raisins
1   large can chunked pineapple, drained
1   cup molasses or maple syrup

Cook beans in fresh water till skins burst. Drain. Mix all ingredients and put in baking pot. Bake, covered, 3 to 4 hours, in moderate oven, adding pineapple and bean juice when mixture needs more moisture. Uncover for the last hour.

TOMATO-CORN BAKE

2   cups corn cut fresh from the cob
3   tomatoes, sliced
1   green pepper, chopped
1   green onion, chopped
3   tablespoons oil
    Dash of curry powder
½   cup grated cheese

Mix all but the cheese together and put in baking dish. Sprinkle with the cheese. Bake in moderate oven for half an hour.

RICE

There are many ways to cook rice and just as many ways not to cook it. Some cooks start with cold water; some with hot; and some with oil in a wok. Some wash the rice before cooking; some do not. Some soak the rice overnight to cut the cooking time. Some cook covered; some uncovered. Some let stand after cooking; some serve immediately. Some serve soggy gray globs of rice; some can make each granule fluffy and white.

Here is advice from two old-timers and then some of the ways I cook rice.

> I was taught by an Indian officer to boil rice for curry so that each grain stood separately from the other when it was cooked. "Now," said he, "here's a tea-cupful of rice; wash it well. Take another cup of the same size; measure it twice with boiling water; add a pinch of salt; make the water boil quickly; throw in the rice, and after it is boiled on a slow fire (reckon 20 minutes)

there will be water to drain off. Stir up the rice with a fork; turn it into a dish; let it dry 2 or 3 minutes before the fire, and it is done." ELIZABETH WARREN,
My Lady-Help and What She Taught Me, 1877

I venture to say not one in ten of the readers of the *Cultivator* has even heard of a recipe for so simple a piece of rich cookery. There is none more important. Try it. If it is an improvement, recommend. Put 3 cups of rice into 2 cups of cold water. Set it over a brisk fire, and after it commences boiling, let it stand 8 minutes only—'tis then ready for the table. Instead of being a mass of unwholesome salve, it will have completely absorbed the water, leaving the grains separate, soft and excellent.
SOLON ROBINSON, in *Albany Cultivator,* October, 1837

RICE RECIPE I

1   cup brown rice
2½   cups cold water

Bring to a boil and cook hard 5 minutes. Cover and simmer an hour without lifting lid. Set on back of stove for 10 more minutes. Then serve.

RICE RECIPE II

Wash rice in plenty of cold water until water is clear. Put in pot with water to cover by half an inch. Cover and bring to boil. When water starts to boil, give the rice one stir so that no grains stick to bottom. Then cook over moderate heat, with lid on, for 25 minutes or until water is all absorbed. Pull to back of stove and leave covered for 10 minutes.

BAKED RICE

1   onion, chopped
1   tablespoon vegetable oil
2   cups brown rice
1   cup chopped parsley
1   garlic clove, minced
1   teaspoon sesame seeds

Sauté the onion in the oil in skillet. Add the dry rice, parsley, garlic and seeds. Sauté again. Put in covered casserole with 3 cups boiling water. Bake 2 hours in hot oven.

MEXICAN RICE

2   cups brown rice
1   onion, chopped
2   cloves garlic, chopped
¼   cup oil
3   tomatoes, chopped
4   cups soup stock
¼   cup chopped parsley

Cover rice with hot water and let stand for half an hour. Drain. Sauté onion and garlic in the oil for 10 minutes. Add tomatoes and sauté 10 minutes. Add rice and soup stock. Boil 15 minutes, then cover and simmer till all liquid is absorbed. Garnish with chopped parsley.

RAISINED RICE

1 cup brown rice
1 cup raisins
2 tablespoons butter
½ cup honey

Wash the rice and put into 3 cups of cold water. Bring to boil and cook, covered, for half an hour. Add raisins, butter and honey. Serve immediately.

MILLET CASSEROLE

2 cups millet
1 onion, chopped
3 stalks celery, chopped
1 green pepper, sliced
2 tomatoes, chopped
2 tablespoons parsley, chopped
1 tablespoon oil
½ cup grated cheese

Cook millet in boiling water to cover for 15 minutes. When millet is done, mix everything but cheese in a casserole. Sprinkle with grated cheese and bake for half an hour in a hot oven.

CURRIED LENTILS AND RICE

½ cup brown rice
1 onion, chopped

    2 garlic cloves, minced
    2 tablespoons oil
    ½ teaspoon curry powder
    1 tablespoon lemon juice
    ½ cup lentils
    4 stalks spinach, chopped
   12 cherry tomatoes

Sauté rice, onion, and garlic in oil till sizzling. Add curry, then 2 cups water, the lemon juice, and lentils. Cover and simmer until tender (about half an hour). Stir in the chopped raw spinach. Bring to a boil and then remove from the stove. Serve in individual bowls topped with a scattering of small red tomatoes.

LENTIL CURRY

   2 cups lentils
   2 teaspoons curry powder
   4 cups water
   3 onions, sliced
   3 tomatoes, sliced
   1 tablespoon oil
   ¼ cup peanut butter
   ¼ teaspoon cumin seed or turmeric
     Handful of chopped parsley

Cook lentils and curry in 4 cups water till lentils are just tender. Meanwhile, sauté onions and tomatoes in oil. Stir both mixtures together. Stir in the peanut butter and cumin. Heat and serve with sprinkled parsley.

ANITA'S CURRY

6 onions, sliced
1 tablespoon oil
4 tomatoes, chopped
1 cup raisins
1 teaspoon honey
½ teaspoon curry powder
  Handful of shelled peanuts

Sauté onions in oil. Add cut-up tomatoes, then raisins, then curry, and last of all the peanuts. Serve with rice.

KASHA QUICKIE

2 cups buckwheat groats
5 cups boiling water
1 tablespoon butter
½ teaspoon salt

Slowly stir kasha into boiling water. Stir for a few minutes. Add butter and let pan simmer, covered, 10 minutes, or until water is absorbed. If cooked in double boiler, it need not be watched, but takes longer.

BUCKWHEAT DINNER DISH

2 onions, chopped
4 carrots, grated or chopped
2 cups buckwheat groats
1 garlic clove, minced

222

Pinch of sea salt
4 cups water
2 tablespoons butter

Simmer onions and carrots in oiled heavy pot. Add buckwheat, garlic, sea salt and water. Bring to boil, then simmer, covered, till liquid is absorbed. Serve hot, with dots of butter.

*E*ATE not your bread too stale, nor eate it hot. Yet let it be well bak't or eate it not.

SIR JOHN HARYNGTON,
The Schoole of Salerne, 1607

Cake is a kind of bread of light nourishment and in my opinion not agreeable for mankind.

DR. VENNER,
Via Recta ad Vitam Longam, 1622

The great quantities of the Confectioners Hodge-podge, the Cakes, the Buns, the Gingerbread, etc., all which do wonderfully indispose the Stomach, and prepare matter for the Regiment of Diseases.

THOMAS TRYON,
The Good House-wife Made a Doctor, 1692

All pastry is an abomination. It is one of the most indigestible substances in the world. If we could see the contents of the stomach, an hour after the mass is swallowed, we should find it to be mere paste. . . . The best use which can be made of cherry pies is to throw them away.

WILLIAM A. ALCOTT,
The Young Mother, 1836

Doughnuts are very rich; do not give them to children.

DR. OLDCOOK, *Receipt Book,* 1847

On the plain household bread his eye did not dwell; but he surveyed some currant tea-cakes, and condescended to make choice of one.

CHARLOTTE BRONTË, *Shirley,* 1849

There are more women who know how to make good cake than good bread.

HARRIET BEECHER STOWE, *House & Home Papers,* 1865

Not that the pleasures of eating are to be wholly despised. No. Far be it from me to scorn the pleasures of the palate. I would by no means consider it wicked to eat, semi-occasionally, a bit of cake; and there may be times in the year when even pie would be in order.

A.M. DIAZ,
Papers Found in the School Master's Trunk, 1875

Pastry should never be a daily occurrence. When it is rich, it is both good and indigestible; when it is cheap, it is bad and still more indigestible.

CHRISTINE TERHUNE HERRICK, *Housekeeping Made Easy,* 1888

224

13

Baked Goods
& Over-Starching

M UCH dough-bake I praise not."[1] Elbert Hubbard
once said, "If I had two loaves of bread I would
sell one to buy a hyacinth to feed my soul." If *I* had two
loaves of bread I would sell both to buy two hyacinths.

Scott and I eat little bread, or any starchy foods. Cereals we eat at only one meal a day, at most. They form
only a small part of our diet. Our main emphasis is on
fresh green vegetables. Who would prefer a doughnut to
an apple, or a cracker to a crunchy leaf of cabbage? Not
we; though I know that millions would.

Starch consumption is almost universal throughout
the world, being found in the seeds, pith or tubers of all
plants except fungi. Rice is 76 percent starch; corn is 56
percent; wheat, 55 percent; millet, 55 percent; barley,
46 percent; rye, 45 percent; peas, 40 percent; lentils, 40
percent; beans, 38 percent; oats, 36 percent; yams, 35
percent; and the lowly potato (which so many people

[1]Thomas Tusser, *Five Hundreth Pointes of Good Husbandrie,* 1557

225

shun "because it is so starchy" and favor bread instead) contains only 18 to 20 percent starch.

None of the above foods are predominant in *our* diet, although we eat some of each at times. We seem to thrive on less pasty substances. Once a month we might eat rice; once a week potatoes, and once a day one of the grains or pulses in some form. However, over most of the world, cereals are a large part of the regular diet, grain being a relatively cheap source of energy and calories.

> Why or when man first ate the seeds of grasses, learned to grind them into flour, mix the flour with water and bake it into bread is not known. Remains of the Swiss lake-dwellers, who lived about 10,000 years ago, show that even then man had developed a baking art. Tomb paintings of ancient Egypt portray not only the planting and harvesting of wheat but grinding, bread mixing and baking as well. Around 100 B.C. there were 258 bakeshops in Rome, and about 100 A.D. Emperor Trajan established a school for bakers. *Encyclopedia Brittanica,* 1964

The best bread we have ever tasted is the black *chorni hleb* of the Russians, the *roggebrot* of the Dutch and the coarse sourdough bread that our grandson-in-law, Peter Schumann, director of the Bread and Puppet Theater, makes and distributes free at his performances. All of these are made of unbolted and unrefined rye. Peter's is extremely coarsely ground, hard as a rock, and must almost be sliced with saw and hammer, but "an excellent article to exercise too sedentary teeth upon,"[2] and very flavorsome. All three breads are real food, not like the white cotton batting displayed (and, I am sorry to say, sold) in American stores. I wouldn't eat their puffy product if they gave it away.

[2]Dr. Russell Thacker Trall, *The New Hydropathic Cook Book,* 1854

The modern methods of processing—purifying (deleting the bran), fine grinding, fine sifting, bleaching, "enriching," adulterating—robs good cereals of their life-giving energy. Bread becomes not the staff of life but the crutch of constipation, illness and death. The heart of the grain is its life-germ, its spark of life, and this is removed to make fine white flour, the bulk ingredient of most commercial breads.

A dead flour is required for bulk storage. Processing a grain to that end results in an incomplete food. Flour products are nutritionally inferior to whole, unground-up, grain foods. Whole grains, such as wheat, buckwheat, oats, millet, barley, brown rice, corn, supply vital minerals, proteins, a little fat and vitamins (especially B complex). They have a high nutritional value *if* used in whole form.

Vegetarians, dropping meat, tend to fill up with too much starch. This leaves them no more healthy than meat-eaters, with constipation, indigestion, colds, catarrhs, coughs and chest complaints to plague them. Eating sparingly of breads, cakes, crackers, cookies, macaroni, spaghetti, anything largely starch, is a far step on the road to good health.

Instead of bread, Scott and I eat the whole unbroken unground grains. Buckwheat and millet need only a few minutes on the stove, in boiling water, to be ready to eat. In the case of wheat, which is an exceedingly hard grain, the berries must be soaked overnight and boiled in plenty of water for several hours.

One of the objections I have to making bread is the trouble and time it takes. The elaborate directions bore me. Enthusiastic friends say baking bread is far less complicated than baking a cake—but why bake a cake? People invariably say, "But bread is so simple to make," and then show me a recipe that takes up a page and a half in print, and an hour or more of their time. My objections are the same for pies, cookies and muffins.

Now, all these things may gratify the palate; but the point is, are they worth the price that is paid for them? I see that the rows of pies on the buttery shelves, the mounds of cake, the stacks of doughnuts, do not come there by any magical sleight of hand, but are wrought out of the very life of poor Mrs. Fennell, our cook.

A.M. DIAZ, *Papers Found in the School Master's Trunk,* 1875

Sisters, take account of your baking-day processes, and see if you do not do much more baking than is consistent with the good digestion of your family, or your own health, and having made up your mind wherein you can reduce that day's work, talk the matter over with your husbands, and see if they do not very sensibly and kindly agree to do with less fresh bread and fewer pies and cakes, if it will give you immunity from extra work.

EMMA C. HEWITT, *Queen of Home,* 1888

Baked goods are usually mixtures of lifeless articles: ground-up and processed grains, salt, sugar, yeast, baking powder being mixed together into a sticky dough, and heated in the oven till it is baked to death. Bread is also unhealthy in that it is usually laden down with butter, cheese, jam, honey, mayonnaise, or other extras, bread being just the background. Would it be eaten so plentifully without the fullsome additions? If hungry, why not eat crunchy celery stalks, or radishes, or apples, instead of bread?

It's so easy to stuff soft bread down the gullet. Bread needs so little mastication and slides down with minimal effort. If new and hot, it forms a heavy indigestible doughball in your mouth and stomach. Shakespeare's King Henry V "gets him to bed crammed with distressful bread."

228

It may well be that the greatest disease of the Middle Ages was neither leprosy nor St. Anthony's Fire, but the constantly sluggish condition of bodily metabolism due to a diet too largely made up of bread.   E. PARMALEE PRENTICE,
Hunger and History, 1939

Bread on the whole is not a very satisfactory food, because it is very acid and on this account is apt to ferment and cause flatulence, especially when eaten with fruit, so in those inclined to flatulence the amount of bread in the day should be limited to small quantities. I have often seen flatulence disappear after cutting down bread and fluids.   K.G. HAIG,
Health Through Diet, 1913

Henry Miller caustically commented that American bread, "the staff of our unsavory and monotonous life, is so unpalatable that under no circumstances should it be fed even to birds. The birds of North America are already on the decline, and this would do them in."

Friends in Queensland, Australia, have sent me a recipe that seems surpassing good and plenty easy to make. I'll paraphrase. Soak wheat seed overnight (or a day and a night) and sprout it. Put the sprouts in a blender or through a meat-grinder. Pour in molasses till it is "soupy." Then grind enough fresh grain until it makes a flour for the sprout mixture. Put into oiled tins and bake, slowly. "It's a very slow heat and it also gets a bit of aroma of the wood fire. I'd say we leave it in the oven three or four hours, turning the loaves around. That's the end of the bread. I don't think it can be further simplified, because if you leave out the wheat or the molasses you're down to water."

I have never baked a pie, nor a cake, nor will I ever. Wait, *once* I made a cake, half a lifetime ago, and it proved so rich and delectable that I never made another. I called it *Helen's Dare-Devil Cake!*

In a large saucepan blend 1 cup molasses and ½ cup water. Cook over low heat, stirring constantly, until mixture comes to a boil. Add a pound of raisins; bring to a boil again. Reduce heat and simmer 5 minutes. Remove from heat and stir in half a pound of finely cut dates and a pound of mixed candied fruit. Set aside. Cream together 1 cup butter and 1 ¼ cups sugar. Blend in 6 eggs, one at a time. Sift together 2 ¼ cups flour, ½ teaspoon baking soda and spices (a teaspoon cinnamon, a teaspoon nutmeg, ½ teaspoon allspice and ½ teaspoon ground cloves). Add to butter mixture alternately with ½ cup orange juice. Stir in the molasses-fruit mixture. Stir in 3 cups chopped nuts. Turn into greased small loaf pans. Bake for 3 hours or until done.

Now my reputation as an anti-cooking cook is gone. But it was a good fruitcake and served as Christmas presents to all the neighbors. A small slice was as good as a meal in halting hunger.

The culinary abominations that are layered, soft and sweet, with gooey icing, seen at ladies' bake sales, are not prescribed for healthful living. For quality, good taste and good health they are at the bottom of the food ladder. I would rather have a loaf of Peter Schumann's black rye bread than any cake ever made, and that includes my one solo performance.

Cakes are essentially forms of refined, intensified, sweetened, flavoured, and ornamented bread. They are baked for the joyful occasion, the social gathering, the feast.   J.L.W. THUDICUM,
The Spirit of Cookery, 1895

Layer cake doesn't interest me especially. After all, it's only an excuse for the frosting.   HAROLD LLOYD,
The Stag Cook Book, 1922

WAYFARER'S BREAD

1   cup wheat berries (wheat seed)
    Water
    Sesame or sunflower seeds

Soak the wheat berries overnight in plenty of water. In the morning, pour off the water and put berries in a covered bowl without any water. Let stand, and rinse with water twice a day. Within two days, the berries ought to sprout double the size of the wheat seed. Put the sprouted berries through a coarse grinder. (Wash the grinder immediately after using, or you'll have a horrendous gluteny mess to clean out.) Shape the wheat dough with your wet hands into small flat loaves about an inch high. Scatter some sesame (or sunflower) seeds on a baking sheet so that bread doesn't stick to the pan. Bake the loaves till brown in a hot oven.

Variations: This bread can also be made of rye seed. Raisins or crumbled dried herbs or cut-up dates or nuts may be added to the dough.

PETER SCHUMANN'S RYE BREAD

Grind any quantity of rye berries fairly coarse. Mix with warm water to a porridge consistency. Let it sit in a warm place for 2 to 3 days, by which time it will ferment and make sourdough. Grind an equal quantity of rye berries and mix with the sourdough. Add some salt and enough warm water to be able to knead very vigorously for 20 to 30 minutes. Cover and let sit for an hour. Knead again, then form loaves by lightly rolling on a floured board. Bake 1 ½ hours in a hot oven. The crust will be *hard*. Cut very thin with a sharp, strong knife. The bread is better after 2 days and will keep for months.

UNCOOKED FRUIT CAKE

1 quart raw wheat berries, ground fine
1 coconut, grated, and its milk
½ pound raisins
¼ pound citron rind, grated or chopped

Stir together. Then press into a pie plate by hand. Keep in cool place, or eat at once.

INDIAN CAKE

1 cup cornmeal
2 cups wholewheat flour
1 cup maple or raw sugar
½ cup raisins, soaked overnight
½ cup chopped nuts
1 cup butter
3 tablespoons molasses

Mix dry ingredients together. Melt butter over fire. Pour over the flour mixture and stir, adding molasses. Rinse out butter kettle with a few tablespoons of boiling water, and add it until the whole mixture is pourable into well-greased pie plate. Bake in hot oven till brown.

DUTCH ROGGEBROT

    4   cups rye meal
    1   cup cracked wheat
    ¼   cup wheat germ
    1   tablespoon caraway seed
    1½ teaspoons sea salt
    2   tablespoons oil
    2   tablespoons honey or molasses
    3   cups boiling water

Mix dry ingredients together. Stir in the moist. Cover and set aside all night. Depending on consistency, add more flour in the morning if necessary to make a solid loaf. Bake in hot oven 4 hours in covered pan placed in pan of hot water, keeping the water pan full.

PHILIP LOVELL'S O-SO-EASY BREAD

    2   tablespoons honey dissolved in cup warm water
    1   package or cake of yeast, dissolved in cup warm water
    ¾   pound wholewheat flour

Add the honey and yeast to the flour. Stir thoroughly for 3 minutes. Add a handful more flour if necessary to make a smooth firm dough. It need not be kneaded. Put in long bread pan and place in a warm place (not the oven) for 45 minutes. Then bake in a hot oven for an hour.

FLAT BREAD

2   cups wholewheat flour
    Pinch of sea salt

Mix together, then add sufficient cold water to make a thick batter. Pour ¼"-thick onto hot oil-covered frying pan. Cook on both sides till crisp brown.

Variation: Same ingredients, but use *boiling* water to mix to a very dry dough. Roll out ¼"-thick on floured board. Cut in squares and bake in hot oven, turning to brown both sides.

GREENCORN BREAD

When corn is green, too hard for boiling but still too soft for grinding into meal, try grating it on a coarse grater. Add a bit of sea salt to the mixture and form into small loaves with your hands. Bake on a cookie sheet in a hot oven for one-half hour or until brown.

INDIAN CHAPPATIES

Mix any amount of flour in a big bowl with enough cold water to make a stiff dough. Knead it, then break off blobs the size of eggs. Roll them very thin on a floured board. Cook on top of stove on ungreased griddle, or lightly oiled heavy frying pan. Turn, so both sides get brown.

CORN PONE

2 cups cornmeal
1 teaspoon sea salt
¼ cup oil

Mix dry ingredients. Stir in the oil. Add enough cold water to make firm balls with the hands. Flatten into patties and bake in corncake molds or on oiled baking sheet. Bake in hot oven until brown.

UNCOOKED NUT LOAF

1 cup ground almonds
½ cup chopped walnuts
4 tablespoons rolled oats
½ teaspoon sea salt
  Pinch of thyme
  2 to 4 tablespoons cold water

Mix nuts together, then add oats, sea salt and thyme. Moisten gradually with water and form into a loaf. Let stand in a cold place for at least an hour before serving. Slice with sharp knife. This is used as a main course, with vegetables and salad, not as a bread.

CORN BREAD

The best corn bread we ever ate was from meal well-kneaded, with nothing but water and a little salt, and then made into lumps about the size and somewhat the shape of a man's foot, and raked in the embers just like potatoes to roast, and there allowed to remain and cook all night.

Remember the three grand secrets about making good corn bread: Never grind your meal very fine; always have it fresh-ground, and never fear baking it too much. All corn bread should be cooked a long time.　　　　SOLON ROBINSON,
Facts for Farmers, 1866

WHEATIES

1　cup margarine
3　cups wholewheat flour
1　cup cottage cheese

Mix softened margarine with the flour. Blend well with your hands. Stir in the cottage cheese. It should become a dryish though sticky dough. Roll it out on a floured board and cut in small thin squares or circles, or make thin patties with your hands. Bake on oiled cookie pan in hot oven till brown on both sides.

OUR VERMONT JOURNEY CAKES

2　cups cornmeal
2　cups wholewheat flour
1　cup rolled oats
1　cup rolled wheat
½　cup wheat germ
1½　teaspoons sea salt
1　cup chopped nuts (optional)
½　cup raisins (optional)

2 cups blackstrap molasses or dark maple syrup
1 quart buttermilk or sour milk

Mix all dry ingredients together in big bowl, then add liquid. Add enough rinse water from milk bottle to make mixture moist enough to drop from spoon, yet it should hold shape on dropping. Spoon into individual greased corncake molds and bake in hot oven for half an hour. Turn cakes over so that the bottom browns too.

Variation: We now make this without the milk but with added soy sauce (3 tablespoons) or oil (3 tablespoons).

PEANUT CORNMEAL CRISPS

1 cup peanut butter
1 cup cold water
1 cup cornmeal

Cream the peanut butter with the water. Warm in pan on stove. Stir in the cornmeal. Beat thoroughly. Add more water if necessary to form small thin cakes. Drop from wooden spoon onto oiled cookie sheet. Bake in moderate oven for one-half hour or till browned.

CRUSTY CARROT CROAKERS

6 cups grated carrots (I use the residue from making carrot juice)
1 cup cornmeal

1   cup wheat germ
½   cup ground sunflower seeds
1   cup rolled oats
1   cup wholewheat flour
1   tablespoon sea salt
    Handful of any dried herb
3   tablespoons molasses
4   tablespoons oil
    Soup stock or water

Mix together all ingredients, adding just enough soup
stock or water to moisten sufficiently to make rolls with
the hands. Bake in individual corncake molds in hot
oven for an hour. Turn cakes over so that bottoms brown
too.

ANNIE'S MUFFINS

1½   teaspoons active yeast
1   cup bran
½   cup soy milk or water
1   tablespoon oil
2   cups wholewheat flour

Dissolve yeast in ½ cup warm water. Allow the bran to
soften in ½ cup warm soy milk or warm water for 5
minutes. Add oil and mix in yeast. Stir in the flour and
bran until dough becomes somewhat elastic. Allow the
dough to rise for 15 minutes in a warm place. Drop
tablespoonfuls of dough into muffin tins or onto greased
pie plates. Bake in very hot oven for 20 minutes.

CARROT COOKIES

2 cups wholewheat flour
2 cups grated carrots
½ cup chopped nuts
½ cup shredded coconut
  Dash of sea salt
½ cup oil
½ cup maple syrup or honey
  Dash of lemon juice

Mix the dry ingredients. Add the moist. Stir. Drop by spoonfuls on oiled cookie sheet. Bake in hot oven till brown.

BANANA COOKIES

3 tablespoons honey
8 tablespoons soy oil
1 ripe banana, mashed
2 cups wholewheat flour
½ cup water or fruit juice
½ cup raisins, soaked overnight

Mix honey and oil together. Add banana. Work flour in with a wooden spoon or by hand. Add the liquid. Add the raisins. Drop by spoonfuls on oiled cookie pans and bake in moderate oven till browned.

BUCKWHEAT CRUNCHIES

1   cup buckwheat groats
1   cup wholewheat flour
2   tablespoons honey
1   tablespoon molasses
2   tablespoons oil

Combine dry ingredients. Add the moist. Knead or stir to make stiff dough. Roll on floured board, then cut in squares. Bake on oiled cookie sheet in hot oven till brown.

OATMEAL CHEWIES

2   cups rolled oats
2   cups wholewheat flour
1   ripe banana, mashed
½   cup raisins, soaked overnight
1   cup honey
1½   cups cold water or apple cider
2   teaspoons lemon juice
2   tablespoons molasses

Mix together dry ingredients. Mix the moist. Add moist to dry. Stir together. Drop by spoonfuls on oiled pans and bake in moderate oven till browned.

PEANUT BUTTER WAFERS

2   tablespoons peanut butter
½   cup honey
2   tablespoons peanut oil
1   cup rolled oats
1   cup wholewheat flour
½   teaspoon vanilla

Mix peanut butter, honey and oil. Then emulsify them with ¼ cup of water. Add the rolled oats and flour and vanilla flavoring. Mix well. Drop from spoon on oiled cookie sheet. Bake in hot oven till brown.

*B*UT I have sweeter stuffe to tell you of. After Dinner, comes the real Banquet: enters the Confectioner, who will shew you such Rarities, that therein Art seems to out-doe herself. SIR THEODORE MAYERNE, *Excellent & Approved Receipts & Experiments in Cookery,* 1658

Let not the sugred baites of Sardonicall sinne allure your Palates.
WILLIAM VAUGHAN,
Directions for Health, 1600

Blanchmange, custards and trifles, and the endless and useless collection of pretty playthings for the palate. DR. WILLIAM KITCHINER, *The Cook's Oracle,* 1817

It is as much as one's life is worth, almost, in this day of excitement, and exciting things, to keep the young away from confectionery. Common sugar and plain molasses are tempting enough, and bad enough; but when we go beyond these, and present to the eager juvenile appetite the more fashionable preparations of the modern confectioner, it is with exceeding great difficulty that they are kept within the bounds of reason and experience.
WILLIAM A. ALCOTT,
The Mother in Her Family, 1838

While the preparation of soups and gravies is left to ruder and stronger hands, the delicate fingers of the lady of the household are best suited to mingle the proportions of exquisite desserts. It is absolutely necessary to the economy of the household that this art should form a part of every lady's education.
A Boston Lady, *The Dessert Book,* 1872

One charming thing about dessert is that ladies can make them: they do not flush the face or derange the white apron. They are pleasant things to dally with—milk and eggs, and spice and sugar. To cook a heavy dinner in hot weather, to wash the dishes afterward, this is sober prose, and by a very dull author. But to make the dessert, this is poetry. M.E.W. SHERWOOD, *The Art of Entertaining,* 1892

"I must say I enjoy an ice at dinner," said Lady Considine. "I know the doctors abuse them, but I notice they always eat them when they get the chance."
MRS. W.G. WATERS, *The Cook's Decameron,* 1920

242

14

Desserts & Other
Delicious Delights

W HEN we moved to Maine in 1953, our nearest
neighbor on Spirit Cove was an unkempt, dishev-
eled, unprepossessing old man who lived in a tumble-
down disorderly house. His intelligence, native knowledge and his constant bright observations made him
good company. He often came over for a meal. When
satisfied, even though pressed to eat more, he invariably
replied with an old-world courtesy, "Thank you. I've had
an ample sufficiency." According to common custom,
dessert is usually served after a meal when the partici-
pants at table have already had an ample sufficiency.

A dessert is eaten not from need but because it tastes
good. The temptation is too great to be resisted. A serving of cake, pudding, pie or ice cream is sometimes followed by a second or even a third helping. I have eaten
such desserts, but not if I were given the choice of a bowl
of ripe red cherries or a bunch of grapes or a juicy pineapple. Fruits are a perfect food, requiring little or no
preparation, cooking, or seasoning. They contain many
of the essential minerals, vitamins and nutrients. If des-

sert *is* taken, fruits and nuts would be more desirable. "With nuts and figs I crowned the cheerful board," said Horace in 30 B.C.

> As for desserts, I am no great friend to them. I think they are unwholesome from being unnecessary. At any rate, I would have them in great moderation, and confined to a few kinds of ripe fruit. Preserved fruits are in my opinion cloying after dinner, and I believe injurious to the digestion of a substantial meal, and confectionery I think still worse. Desserts are made instruments of show, and a perpetual source of temptation to excess.
>
> A Bon Vivant, *The Art of Dining,* 1874

The philosopher Descartes, when a caviling Marquis exclaimed, "What! Do you philosophers eat dainties?" replied, "Do you think Providence made good things only for fools?" So, I can touch on the subject of ice cream, a general favorite of young and old, and a dainty on which I occasionally fall from grace. In my childhood it was made at home solely of cream, fruit and sugar, and was laboriously cranked in a wooden freezer made to hold chopped ice and salt. It was a very special dessert rather than a common one, as it is today, and was reserved for appropriate occasions. When Scott was courting me (if such a fancy phrase can describe our "going together") he made a most delicious banana ice cream: one part cream, one part milk, one part crushed fruit, and sweetened to taste. We've rarely had it since.

Foods preserved and sweetened to titillate the taste cannot be considered in the same rank as fresh foods. Perhaps the greatest harm from eating sweetened foods is that it supplants the plainer, less adorned but more substantial and important foods. Fruits are so plentiful and so good that we do not need concentrated sweets, which are enticing but of doubtful value to the body's well-being.

I know a dentist who calls candy "the dentist's delight," and has a sticker on his ceiling, where patients can ponder it while undergoing his probing: "Support your local dentist. Eat more candy."

A prohibition of the sale of candies would put fifty percent of all the dentists out of business within three years.

DR. A.F. REINHOLD,
Nature Versus Drugs, 1898

Having uttered many sour notes on sugar and sweets, let me now tell you how I make some jams and candies, using natural sweetening and not refined sugar. Most jams that I make nowadays (and they are very few) are uncooked—just raspberries, strawberries, blueberries, blackberries from the garden, mashed in a bowl and sweetened with stirred-in honey. These I bottle cold and put in the freezer.

I have made cooked jams in the past and can pass on some handy hints. Use fruits on the unripe side; it contains more pectin and will solidify quicker. To aid this thickening, you might scrape a small raw potato into each boiling kettle as it nears the end of cooking. For those whom this practice affrights or repulses, scrape a small unripe green apple into each kettle. It fulfills the same purpose.

Before making jams rub a small blob of butter over the whole inside of the pan, including the top edge. It will prevent scorching and boiling over.

Crush your fruit till juicy before putting on the stove. Then bring to the boil slowly before gradually adding sugar or whatever sweetening you will use.

There is no need to paraffin your jars. Fill to the top and tighten the lid. Then turn the jars upside down for a few minutes and then put upright in a pan of cool water and 'twill seal.

For best success, make jams on a clear dry day.

A favorite sport for cooks is making relishes or pickles. In my early cooking venturing, while I was still flinging foods around indiscriminately and had not settled down to my present sober, frugal pace, I made many pickled concoctions. I felt like a witch over a cauldron, adding cloves, allspice, cinnamon, dill, with vinegar and sugar, to beets or cabbage or apples or cucumbers.

My mixtures tasted good to me and were fun to make, but I came to realize the resultant jumble was unwholesome if not poisonous to our systems. Scott stopped eating them, and I stopped relishing the relishes. One old-time book, after giving a recipe for spiced cucumbers, convinced me with its recommendation: "After having prepared them in fine style—throw them away." I don't throw them away. I just don't make them anymore: those "passionate desire foods that are bitter, sour, saline, over-hot, pungent, dry and burning, and which produce pain, grief and sickness. The foods that augment vitality, energy, vigour, health, joy and cheerfulness, delicious, bland, substantial and agreeable, are dear to the pure."[1]

Condiments only create a false hunger, a *desire* for food. True hunger, a *need* for food, has been said to be the best pickle.

> Denyse, kyng of Sicilie, when he had eaten potage whiche a Cooke of Lacedemonia had made, said that the meate did not delite him. The Cook answered, it was no mervaile, for it lacked spices. When the kyng asked what spices, he answered: Labour, sweate, hunger, and thyrst, for with suche manner of stuffe the meate of the Lacedemonians was ever prepared.
>
> SIR THOMAS ELYOT,
> *The Bankette of Sapience*, 1545

[1] *The Bhagavad-Gita*, 5th century B.C.

However, from my misspent youth, here are some holdovers in the way of desserts, which are not too unwholesome.

APPLESAUCE

1 cup maple syrup
½ cup water
8 apples, unpeeled, cored

Bring syrup and water to a rolling boil. Cut up apples into sixths. Add to the boiling syrup. Stir up, and then let simmer until apple slices are barely tender and not mashed.

BAKED APPLES

6 apples, quartered and cored
½ cup maple syrup
2 tablespoons butter

Do not peel the apples unless the skins are tough. Place the apples in a baking dish. Add enough water to cover the bottom of the dish. Add the maple syrup and scatter bits of butter over the apples. Bake for half an hour in a hot oven. Serve warm.

APPLICIOUS

1 quart applesauce
3 ripe bananas, mashed

1 cup sour cream
3 tablespoons maple syrup
   Dash of lemon juice
½ cup chopped walnuts, pecans or other nuts

In a large bowl, mix the applesauce with the bananas, sour cream, maple syrup and the lemon juice. Spoon the mixture into individual bowls. If not serving right away, store in the refrigerator. Just before serving, sprinkle the chopped nuts over each portion.

CRAN-APPLESAUCE

2 cups fresh cranberries
3 cups peeled, sliced apples
2 cups orange sections
½ cup maple syrup

Wash the cranberries and drain well, removing any damaged berries. Place one-half of the berries in a 2-quart casserole. Top with one-half of the apple slices and one-half of the orange sections. Repeat the layers, using the remaining fruit. Pour the syrup over the fruit. Bake, covered, in a moderate oven for 30 to 45 minutes. Serve warm or chilled.

RASPBERRY APPLESAUCE

2 cups fresh raspberries
4 cups peeled, cubed apples
½ teaspoon cinnamon
1–2 tablespoons honey, or to taste

FRIED BANANAS

6   peeled bananas
½   cup maple syrup

Arrange the bananas in a large skillet, and pour the syrup on top. Place the skillet over medium heat and cook the bananas, turning occasionally, until the maple syrup begins to candy. Serve hot.

BANANA TOFU PUDDING

3   very ripe bananas
2   cakes tofu
3   tablespoons maple syrup
    Dash of cinnamon or nutmeg

Slice the bananas and place them in a blender. Cut the tofu into smaller cubes and add to the bananas, along with the maple syrup. Blend everything together until smooth. Serve the mixture in bowls, and sprinkle the cinnamon or nutmeg on top.

SNOW ICE CREAM

6   ripe bananas, sliced
½   cup maple syrup
½   cup powdered soymeal or powdered milk
    Dash of vanilla
1½ quart bowlful of new-fallen snow

Place the bananas, syrup and soymeal or powdered milk in the container of a blender or food processor, and blend or process until smooth. (The mixture can also be beaten together by hand.) Add the vanilla. Go out, get your snow, and add it to the banana mixture, blending thoroughly. Place the mixture in 2 freezer trays, and freeze for at least 2 hours before serving.

SCOTT'S PHILADELPHIA ICE CREAM

2   cups heavy cream
2   cups milk
2   cups crushed fruit (bananas, strawberries, peaches)
1   cup honey or sugar, or to taste

Stir all the ingredients together in a large bowl, and place the mixture in an old-fashioned hand-crank churner if you have one. Churn until the mixture is thickened. If not serving right away, you can transfer the ice cream to a freezer container and freeze it until needed. If you don't have a churner, place the mixture in two or more shallow freezer trays, and freeze for 3 to 4 hours. Stir the mixture occasionally while freezing.

GINGERED PEARS

6   pears, peeled
3   tablespoons lemon juice
2   teaspoons powdered ginger
2   tablespoons honey or maple syrup
½   cup water
½   cup sour cream or plain yogurt

Slice the pears and toss them with the lemon juice, coating well. Place the ginger, honey and water in a small saucepan, and bring to a boil; simmer for 5 minutes. Cool the mixture and pour it over the pears. Serve the pears in individual bowls, topped with the sour cream or yogurt.

FIG-RAISIN DESSERT

20 dried black figs
1 cup raisins
   Water
2 cups sour cream

Place the figs and raisins in a small bowl; add enough water to cover. Let soak overnight. The next day, drain off any excess liquid and serve the fruit topped with the sour cream.

SO SIMPLE BLUES

1 quart fresh blueberries
2 tablespoons maple syrup
¼ cup sour cream

Wash the blueberries, drain and let dry. Place the berries in individual bowls. Pour the syrup evenly over the berries, and spoon the sour cream on top.

BERRY SHERBET

1 quart blueberries, raspberries or strawberries
½ cup maple syrup
1 cup sour cream

Wash the berries and mash them up. Mix the berries with the syrup, and place the mixture in one or two shallow freezer trays. Place the trays in the freezer for at least 2 hours, stirring with a fork once or twice while freezing. In 2 hours the mixture should be stiff enough to serve, or it can be left overnight. Serve the fruit in bowls, topped with a dollop of sour cream.

GREEN GRAPE DESSERT

4 cups seedless grapes
1 cup sour cream or plain yogurt
½ cup honey or maple syrup

Wash the grapes, drain and dry them and place them in a bowl. Combine the sour cream or yogurt with the sweetener, and toss this mixture with the grapes, coating them well. Refrigerate for a few hours or overnight.

CARROT DELISH

1 cup raisins
½ cup lemon or orange juice
4 large carrots, grated
2 very ripe bananas, thinly sliced
1 cup sour cream
Dash of maple syrup or honey, or to taste

In a medium bowl, soak the raisins in the lemon or orange juice for 30 minutes. Add the carrots, bananas, sour cream and sweetener, and stir the mixture together vigorously. Place the mixture in individual serving dishes, and chill if not serving right away.

FRUIT AMBROSIA

2 cups fresh pineapple chunks or 1 large can pineapple chunks, drained
2 navel oranges, peeled and sectioned
½ cup grated coconut
4 tablespoons maple syrup

In a deep dish, place one-half of the pineapple chunks
and one-half of the orange sections. Sprinkle one-half of
the coconut on top. Repeat the layers, using the remaining pineapple, oranges and coconut. Pour the maple
syrup over all. If not serving right away, store in the
refrigerator.

SWEET MILLET

1 cup millet
1 tablespoon cinnamon
1 tablespoon nutmeg
2 cups boiling water
½ cup chopped nuts
½ cup raisins
2 tablespoons honey or maple syrup

Place the millet and spices in a saucepan. Pour the boiling water on top and stir. Simmer for 10 minutes. Add
the nuts, and cook 5 minutes longer. Add the raisins, and
cook 5 minutes more. Serve warm with the honey or
maple syrup.

SEAWEED PUDDING

1   cup dried seaweed
1   jar (12 ounces) homemade jam (strawberry or rasp-
    berry are best)
1   cup sour cream

Wash the seaweed well and place it in a bowl; add
enough water to cover and soak overnight. The next day,
cook the seaweed with the water over medium heat
until soft. Remove from heat and stir in the jam; let the
mixture cool. Just before serving, stir in the sour cream.

DATE DELISH

½   pound brazil nuts, chopped fine
½   pound dates, chopped fine
½   pound raisins

Mix all together and press onto well-buttered cookie
sheet. Put in refrigerator overnight. Next day cut into
thin slices and serve instead of cookies or cake.

PEANUT BUTTER BALLS

3   cups old-fashioned oats
1   cup peanut butter
½   cup water
1½   cups honey
1   teaspoon vanilla
1   cup chopped nuts

Bring oats and peanut butter to boil with ½ cup water. Add honey, vanilla and chopped nuts. Stir well and bring once more to a boil. Cook for a minute or so. Remove from stove and let cool. Spoon onto a buttered plate or pan, and roll into balls.

HANDY CANDY

1   cup ground nuts
¼   cup brewers' yeast
½   cup raw wheat germ
½   cup honey
2   tablespoons peanut oil
½   cup raisins
    Sesame seeds

Mix together all ingredients except sesame seeds. Roll into balls. Coat with sesame seeds.

HONEY TAFFY

2   cups honey
3   tablespoons butter

Boil honey and butter together until a hard ball is formed when dropped from a spoon in cold water, about 20 minutes. Pour onto marble slab or buttered platter. When cool, butter hands and pull the warm candy into lengths until it becomes hard. Then cut or break into desired pieces.

Variations: 1. Substitute the grated peel from 1 lemon and 2 cups of molasses for the honey. 2. Add a cup of chopped nuts at the time the liquid forms a ball in cold water.

CRANBERRY SAUCE

  4   cups cranberries
1½ cups water
  2   cups honey
  1   orange, peeled, seeded and diced

Bring cranberries to boil in 1½ cups water. Cook 5 minutes. Add honey and boil 5 minutes more. Remove from heat, leaving covered in pot to cool. Stir in the orange just before serving.

A PEACHY JAM

3 cups peeled and cubed peaches
1 cup blueberries
1 cup rose hips, halved and cleaned of seeds
1 cup grated green apple
3 cups honey or raw sugar

Cook all the ingredients together until the mixture becomes thick and sheets off a spoon. Takes up to an hour. Pour into hot sterilized jars and seal.

ROSE HIP JAM

6 cups rose hips, halved and cleaned of seeds
1 cup crab apples or tart apples, unpeeled and diced
1 small potato, scrubbed and grated
½ cup lemon juice
3 cups honey

Stir all ingredients together and cook at a rolling boil till mixture sheets off a spoon. Pour into hot sterilized jars and seal.

ORANGE-CARROT MARMALADE

Juice and rind from 2 oranges
Juice and rind from 1 lemon
2 cups grated carrots
2 cups honey or raw sugar

Cut the rind into slivers, cover with cold water and simmer till tender. Add the grated carrots and honey and stir. Add fruit juice and cook at a rolling boil till the mixture is as thick as you like it. Takes about an hour. Pour into hot sterilized jars and seal.

BLUEBERRY-ROSE HIP JAM

1 quart blueberries, mashed with a potato masher
2 cups rose hips, halved and cleaned of seeds
2 green apples, grated
1 small potato, grated
3 cups honey

259

Cook all together at a rolling boil until the mixture is as thick as you want it and sheets off a spoon. This may take about an hour. Pour into hot sterilized jars and seal.

RAW STRAWBERRY JAM

2   quarts strawberries, mashed
1   cup honey, or to taste

Mix strawberries and honey. Put in jars filled within half an inch of the top and store in refrigerator or freezer.

Variation: This recipe serves for raspberries, blueberries and blackberries as well.

TOMATO RELISH

10   tomatoes, quartered
 3   onions, chopped
 1   head celery, chopped (save heart for salad)
 2   green peppers, chopped
 1   cup cider vinegar
 4   tablespoons honey
 ½   teaspoon cinnamon
 ½   teaspoon ground cloves
 ½   teaspoon sea salt

Mix all together. Cook 2 hours. Pack in sterile pints.

UNCOOKED CARROT RELISH

  1 cup grated carrot
 ½ cup chopped green pepper
 ½ cup chopped celery
 ¼ cup minced onion
  2 tablespoons vinegar
  2 tablespoons honey

Combine all and let stand (in refrigerator) to season until used.

GREEN TOMATO CHUTNEY

  1 pound green tomatoes, chopped
 ½ pound onions, chopped
 ½ pound honey
 ½ pound raisins
  1 pint cider vinegar
  1 tablespoon sea salt

Simmer all together till thickish. Bottle hot in sterilized jars.

ZUCCHINI PICKLE

 ¼ cup honey
  2 teaspoons celery seed
  1 teaspoon mustard
  1 teaspoon sea salt
  1 quart vinegar

4   quarts zucchini, sliced, unpeeled
1   quart onions, sliced

Bring honey, celery seed, mustard and sea salt to boil in the vinegar. Pour boiling mixture over zucchini and onions. Let stand an hour. Bring to boil and simmer for 5 minutes. Put into sterilized jars and keep for winter use.

CUCUMBER PICKLE WITHOUT SALT

Pick and wash any number of small cucumbers and pack in sterile but cold glass jars. Fill jars with cold cider vinegar. Seal tight. Keep in cool place. Use during winter. Vinegar can be reused.

NASTURTIUM PICKLE

Pick and save plenty of nasturtium seeds before they get too large and hard. Put in sterile jars. Fill jars with cider vinegar, a few cloves and a pinch of sea salt. Keep in cellar till wanted.

UNCOOKED ONION RELISH

1   cucumber, peeled and finely chopped
1   onion, chopped
1   tablespoon chopped parsley
1   tablespoon chopped chives

Mix together and moisten with French dressing (2 parts oil to one part vinegar). Keep in refrigerator until used.

CRANBERRY RELISH

2 apples, unpeeled, chopped
4 cups cranberries
1 lemon, juice and rind
2 oranges, juice and rind
  Honey, maple syrup, or raw sugar

Grind all in fine grinder and add maple syrup, honey or raw sugar to taste. Store in refrigerator and use within a day or two.

BEETROOT PICKLE

Boil the unpeeled roots till they are tender (forkable). Put them in cold water and rub off skins. Cut them in thin slices, or in cubes, and bottle them. Meanwhile, boil some vinegar (as much as you think will cover them in their bottles), adding a little sliced ginger and mace. Pour liquid over beets and screw on covers. Keep in refrigerator and use ad lib.

ITALIAN SAUCE

2 onions, chopped
4 garlic cloves, chopped
4 tablespoons olive oil
2 tomatoes, chopped
  Handful of fresh basil, chopped

Sauté onions and garlic in oil till soft. Add tomatoes, basil and salt. Bottle in sterile jars and keep in refrigerator till used.

QUICK TOMATO SAUCE

1   onion, chopped
½   cup olive oil
4   tomatoes, chopped
1   teaspoon oregano
¼   teaspoon cumin seed
¼   teaspoon paprika
½   teaspoon sea salt

Sauté onion in oil. Add all else and bring to rolling boil. Cover and simmer for half an hour. Use on lentils, rice or nut loaf.

VEGETABLE CURRY SAUCE

8   tomatoes, diced
6   onions, chopped
1   cup raisins
¼   teaspoon curry powder

Mix all together and cook over moderate heat for 10 to 15 minutes, stirring occasionally. Use as sauce for cooked rice.

Variation: Add 1 can pineapple chunks.

SWEET YOGURT SAUCE

2 cups plain yogurt
   Juice from ½ lemon
2 tablespoons honey

Combine and mix well.

SHARP YOGURT SAUCE

2 cups plain yogurt
2 cloves garlic, finely minced
½ teaspoon sea salt

Combine and blend well. Use for dip or with vegetables.

HOT BLUEBERRY SAUCE

2 cups blueberries
½ cup honey
½ teaspoon cinnamon
¼ teaspoon nutmeg

Mix all together and boil 10 minutes, stirring well while cooking. Spoon the hot mixture over any dessert desired. (Can be used cold too.)

*L*ET his thirst be quenched and nature is satisfied, no matter whence it comes, or whether he drinks in a golden or a silver goblet, or in the hollow of his hand.   SENECA, *Poverty a Blessing*, 60 A.D.

We have sene men and women of great age, and stronge of body, whyche never, or very seldome, dranke other drynke than pure water. . . . Undoubtedly water hathe preemynence above all other lycoures.

SIR THOMAS ELYOT,
The Castel of Helthe, 1534

We have Drinkes brewed with severall Herbs; whereas some of the Drinkes are such, as they are in effect Meat and Drinke both: So that diverse, especially in Age, doe desire to live with them, with little or no Meat, or Bread.

FRANCIS BACON,
New Atlantis, 1635

Water agrees at all Times, with any Age and Constitution. It is a Liquor we little esteem, because 'tis very common; but if we were to consider the great Benefits produc'd by it, we should value it more than an infinite Number of Things who tho' very rare and precious, are not for their Usefulness to be compar'd with it.   DR. M.L. LEMERY,
A Treatise of All Sorts of Foods, 1745

Drinking with any other intent than to give a keener relish to the enjoyment of food is a most swinish and demoralizing practice, inasmuch as it confounds the intellect, inflames the passions, and renders the legs, which may be likened to the under-standings of mankind, incapable of supporting the superincumbent weight of the man or of proceeding in an upright and straightforward course of life.   PRUDENCE SMITH,
Modern American Cookery, 1831

There is no direction in which a woman more needs both scientific knowledge and moral force than in using her influence to control her family in regard to stimulating beverages.   CATHERINE E. BEECHER,
The New Housekeeper's Manual, 1874

I drank at every vine. The last was like the first. I came upon no wine so wonderful as thirst.   EDNA ST. VINCENT MILLAY,
The Harp Weaver, 1923

266

15

Water & Other Beverages

*T*HE usual daily diet should provide most of the liquid needed by the body. If juice fruits and vegetables are consumed, with no added flavoring or seasoning, the need for water or any additional fluid decreases greatly. Neither Scott nor I drink much water, though we have an abundance on flow from a bubbling spring in the woods. We find that without salting our food, and without much cooking, and some raw fruit every day, we do not want a glass of water a week. Perhaps in the hottest part of summer we might drink a glass a day.

It may be put down as a rule from which it is safe never to depart, that every substitute used for pure cold water as a drink, is an injury to health. As a general thing, we drink too much even of water. When the diet is what it should be, and the health is good, there is little or no thirst.   *Journal of Health,* March, 1853

Water is a safe drink for all constitutions, provided it be resorted to in obedience to the dictates of natural thirst only, and not of habit. Unless the desire for it is felt, there is no occasion for its use during a meal.   DR. ANDREW COMBE,
The Principles of Physiology, 1834

Our food should furnish a large proportion of the liquids our systems need, and if it is of a proper quality and in proper quantity, it will do so. Almost everything we eat—fruit and roots especially—abounds with water.   WILLIAM A. ALCOTT,
The Young Housekeeper, 1842

No person who uses good food, and properly masticates it, will suffer by going without drink. Nature has furnished an abundant supply of liquid to mix with our food, if we will wait with patience her movements. This supply is poured forth from the perpetual fountains in the cheeks and elsewhere.
                                        WILLIAM A. ALCOTT,
Ways of Living on Small Means, 1837

Man is the only animal that drinks when he is not thirsty. He drinks at a meal to be able to eat more. He partakes of heavily seasoned food, whether soup or steak or salted cracker, has a sip or two of water or stronger drink to wash it down, then takes more food and more water. He drinks from boredom, to kill time. He drinks to drown sorrow. He drinks for sociability: "The stroke of five demands my social brew. Some cake? A little cream? One lump, or two?"

There are few hours in life more agreeable than the hour dedicated to the ceremony known as afternoon tea.
                                        HENRY JAMES,
The Portrait of a Lady, 1881

We should eat when we are hungry and drink only when we are dry. Our drink should be water, herb teas, or fresh fruit or vegetable juices, not the commercial colas that taste like a muddy river sweetened with blackstrap molasses, or the insipid soft drinks that are flavored sugar-water, and certainly we need not drink the throat-

scorching, stinging, alcoholic liquors that unduly intoxi-
cate.

Coffee is another powerful stimulant not necessary for
healthful living. The temporary lift it gives is followed by
a corresponding depression. The same bad effect results
from cocoa or chocolate, which contains tannin and caf-
feine as does coffee.

An anonymous early nineteenth-century book tells of
substitutes for coffee: "Some use dry brown bread-crusts
and roast them; others soak rye-grain in rum, and roast
it; others roast peas in the same way as coffee. None of
these are very good."[1] "The Chippewa Indians dissolved
maple sugar in cold water, which served as a drink in hot
weather."[2]

Further back in time, the ancients made what was
called a "caudle" "to comfort the stomacke, good for
an old man."[3] It was a sort of warm drink for sick
persons: a mixture of wine or ale with eggs, bread or
gruel, sugar and spices. A "syllabub" was a beverage
made of cream and cider beaten to a froth. "Sweeten
two quarts cream with loaf-sugar. Grate nutmeg into
it, milk youre cow into the liquor very fast, that it
may be very frothy. This is very good for evening en-
tertainments."[4] Other old recipes mention a "posset"
as a sweetened hot milk drink, and "mead," a
honeyed alcoholic drink.

My own home-tried recipes will not include alcoholic
drinks, but here are two descriptive recipes of old-time
beverages; some words of advice on indulging in them.

[1] *The Frugal Housewife,* 1830
[2] Frances Densmore, *Uses of Plants by the Chippewa Indians,* 1928
[3] A Lady, *Temperance Cook Book,* 1841
[4] Thomas Dawson, *The Good Huswife's Jewell,* 1587

To Make All Manner of Fruit Drinkes

You must boile your frute, whether it be apple, cherie, peach, damson, peare, mulberie, or codling, in faire water, and when they be boyled inough, put them into a bowle, and bruse them with a ladle, and when they be cold, straine them, and put in red wine or claret wine, and so season it with sugar, sinammon and ginger. THOMAS DAWSON,
The Good Huswife's Jewell, 1587

Take yee frute full ripe, brus and strain ym and to every gallon of juce put 2 pound sugar; put it in a barrill or pot and boung it close up. Let it stand a month or 5 weeks then bottel it: put in every bottel a lump of sugar; you may make Chirey wine ye same way. *The Receipt Book of a*
Lady of the Reign of Queen Anne, 1711

Cyder is a good and wholesome Liquor enough, provided it be us'd with Moderation; and it may be said that in general it is better for Health than Wine, because its Spirits are not so impetuous, nor so much agitated as those of Wine.
DR. M.L. LEMERY,
A Treatise of All Sorts of Food, 1745

Fresh, sweet cider, bubbling with beauty, scintillating with sunshafts, needs neither poetry nor spiking to recommend it, so evident is its simple wholesomeness to even the wayfaring man, unless he be a fool. RILEY FLETCHER BERRY,
Fruit Recipes, 1919

Following are some of my simple and little-compounded beverages. The easiest way to mix them is in an electric blender. If you do not have one, an old-fashioned egg-beater might do the job, or fill a screw-top bottle half-full and shake vigorously. Beside our blender, we have one other electric gadget that has proved invaluable to us since electricity was run up our road. We have a vegetable juicer, mostly used for our carrot-beet-apple ambrosia that we imbibe at least once a week.

270

We scrub and slice lengthwise a few pounds of carrots, a few pounds of apples and a couple of peeled raw beets. We put them through the vegetable juicer, pour them together in a pitcher and enjoy one of the finest, most nourishing and most delicious juices it has been our good fortune to drink. This is our regular Sunday night supper, with an overflowing bowl of popcorn, after our weekly twenty-four hour fast.

Sip liquids when drinking; do not gulp down. And remember, "Nothing but water is capable of satisfying thirst. Other drinks answer this purpose only in proportion to the quantity of this fluid they contain."[5]

FRESH CARROT JUICE

1   pound carrots
½   pound apples
2   beets

Scrub and wash the carrots. Wash and core the apples, but do not peel. Cut them in quarters. Clean and peel the beets and slice them. Put carrots, apples and beets through juicer.

MULLED CIDER

½   gallon apple cider
1   teaspoon crushed cardamom seeds
½   teaspoon nutmeg

[5]Lyman C. Draper, *A Helping Hand for Town and Country*, 1870

½ teaspoon cinnamon
½ teaspoon ground cloves
½ cup raisins
Honey or maple syrup to taste
A few cranberries or blueberries

Heat cider and all ingredients except the berries. Do not boil. Can be served hot, or you can cool and freeze in cubes and add to more cider or apple juice. Float berries on top when serving.

CASHEW NUT MILK

4 tablespoons cashew nuts, ground
2 glasses cold water
2 ripe bananas
Water to taste

Put the ground cashews in a blender with the cold water. Blend. Add the bananas, some more water and blend again.

HOT SPICED CRANBERRY PUNCH

2 quarts cranberries
2 quarts water
1 cup maple syrup or honey
4 cinnamon sticks
1 teaspoon whole cloves
1 lemon, cut in thin slices
1 cup orange juice
Dash of nutmeg

Cook the cranberries in 2 quarts water till the skins pop. Strain through a sieve or churn in a blender. Add honey or maple syrup, cinnamon, cloves, and boil 2 minutes. Remove from heat and add lemon slices and orange juice. Reheat and serve hot, sprinkled with nutmeg.

FRESH TOMATO JUICE

In Mexico City a few years back I was taken to a very swell bar "to have a drink." I ordered tomato juice, to the chagrin of my host. It came, bright pink, in a huge and beautiful glass. I said, thinking they were putting something over on me, "I ordered tomato juice." "So it is," the waiter said. I sipped and found it truly was, and the most delicious tomato juice I had ever tasted. I was used to it cooked and canned; this was raw, just whirled in a blender.

I now churn up plenty of ripe tomatoes (cut up in quarters but unpeeled) in my blender, and that's it. The only water added is the rinse water from the blender. It is pure juice of the tomato, simple as can be.

An elaborate alternative:

8 ripe tomatoes, quartered
3 stalks celery, chopped fine
1 green onion, chopped fine
  Juice of ½ lemon
  A leaf or two of basil

Churn all in blender and pour into a pitcher, adding rinse water from the blender.

HAYMAKER'S SWITCHEL

Switchel is a summer haytime drink that keeps the scythes moving. Have plenty of it on hand for thirsty throats.

1	quart cold water
½	cup honey
¼	cup vinegar
½	cup molasses
½	teaspoon powdered ginger

Stir up together and dilute to taste with more cold water. A pinch of baking soda will make it foam up like beer or ginger ale.

GREEN MAGIC

1	young cucumber, sliced but unpeeled
1	green pepper, chopped
1	clove garlic, minced
	Juice of 1 lemon
1	quart apple juice or pineapple juice
3	stalks celery with the green leaves
	Handful of mint leaves
	Handful of minced parsley

Buzz in a blender the cucumber, green pepper, garlic and lemon juice, with enough apple juice or pineapple juice to liquefy. Then add the celery, mint and parsley.

Variation: Spinach leaves, beet tops and comfrey can

be added. The idea is to get as much chlorophyll into your system as possible.

ANY ONE-FRUIT JUICE

Liquefy any fresh fruit or berry (peach, pear, strawberries, raspberries or blueberries) in a blender, with honey or maple syrup to sweeten, and cold water to thin.

BANANA DRINK

Put 4 ripe bananas in a blender with a dash of maple syrup or honey. Add enough water to churn into a good drink for two glasses.

Variation: Instead of water, add 1 cup orange juice, ½ cup grapefruit juice and honey to taste. Churn, and add blender rinse water to drink.

ALMOND MILK

Blanch 2 handfuls of almonds by soaking a few minutes in boiling water and squeezing the skins off. Put in a blender with 4 cups water and 2 tablespoons honey or maple syrup. Churn. Strain. Drink the foamy liquid and chew the nut residue.

MOLASSES DRINK

Mix 8 tablespoons soybean powder or powdered milk, 6 tablespoons molasses and 2 cups water. Bring to boil, stirring. Serve hot or cold.

SEAWEED DRINK

Clean a handful of Irish moss or other seaweed. Rinse well and put in a kettle with 2 quarts boiling water. Simmer for half an hour. Strain. Add juice of 2 lemons and juice and rind of 1 orange. Sweeten to taste with honey or maple syrup. Drink hot or cold.

ROSE HIP TEA

Just plain dried rose hips, as described on pages 283–284 in *Storing & Preserving the Good Food*, made into tea, is rather flat and bland, with little flavor. I usually add camomile or mint, in equal proportions, to the dried rose hips (a pinch of each for each person) and then pour on the boiling water.

COCONUT DRINK

Liquefy in blender 2 ripe bananas, 2 cups pineapple juice, and the water from a whole coconut.

GREEN DELIGHT

Put the juice of 2 grapefruits and 1 orange in a blender. Add a handful of chopped parsley and liquefy until parsley colors the drink. Pour into a pitcher. Rinse out the blender with about 1 cup water and pour into drink.

*A*L appulles, eaten sone after that they be gathered, are hard to digest, but being well kepte untyll the wynter, are right holsome.

SIR THOMAS ELYOT,
The Castel of Helthe, 1534

Without helpe of a Mill to make Otemeale fit for our use, some of those good house-wives that delight not to have anything but from hand to mouth may (while their pot doth seethe) go to the barne and rub forth with their hands sufficient for the present time, not willing to provide for tomorrow but let the next day bring it forth.   Gerard's *Herball,* 1596

The Countrey-Man hath not a familie whose necessities must be alwaies furnished out of the shop, nor their table out of the market, but a provident and gainfull familie. His provision is alwaies out of his own store, and agreeable with the season of the yeare.   DON ANTONIO DE GUEVARA,

The Praise & Happiness of the Countrie-Life, 1631

There is nothing which doth more agreeably concern the Senses, than in the depth of Winter to behold the Fruits so fair, and so good, yea better, than when you first did gather them . . . You will taste your Fruit with infinite more gust and contentment than in the Summer itself, when their great abundance and variety rather cloy you than become agreeable. For this reason it is that we essay to teach you the most expedite and certain means how to conserve them all the Winter, even so long as till the New shall incite you to quit the Old.   JOHN EVELYN,

The French Gardiner, 1675

There can be no doubt whatever that by far the most economical plan of supplying a household with necessaries for consumption is to lay in a stock for the week in lieu of purchasing, as but too many do, from hour to hour.

One Who Makes Ends Meet,
Economy for the Single and Married, 1845

Within the necessary limits, one who has his own garden and his own cellar has a decided advantage over his neighbor who must always rely on the merchant.   ANGELO M. PELLEGRINI,

The Unprejudiced Palate, 1948

16

Storing & Preserving the Good Food

W E old-timers (and Scott and I are that, having homesteaded in Vermont for nineteen years and in Maine for twenty-seven) are used to growing our own food and eating it summer and winter. Our larder is stocked from our garden, not from the stores. We live way out on the end of Cape Rosier on a rocky windswept point, sticking out into Penobscot Bay, twenty miles or more from the nearest village with shops and a bank (Blue Hill), and fifty miles or more from a city of size (Bangor). Our excursions to town are few and far between.

Those who live in large towns can run back and forth to the grocer's and supermarkets every other day for food they need. We grow our greens and roots, eat out of the garden in summer, and out of our large cellar and our sun-heated greenhouse in winter.

Generally speaking, stored or preserved foods are not in the same rank as fresh foods. Fresh vegetables from the garden, of course, have the highest nutritive value and are preferable to those preserved, dried, fermented, canned or frozen. But in our New England climate we must work out some method of storage through the cold season.

One of the early means of storage was a pit, lined and covered with hay or straw, held in place by boards and loose earth, and properly ventilated. Located on a knoll so that moisture would not accumulate, such storage pits proved to be reasonably frost-free. On sunny days, even in the middle of winter, one could open up the pits and take a portion of the contents for immediate use.

An alternative was to pick a side-hill location close to the farm buildings, dig a hole into the hill, build a front door and a ventilator. The side-hill location, well-chosen, took care of water accumulation. The part of the storage cellar dug into the side-hill below frost level had the advantage of earth temperatures (in New England, in the forties). The part of the storage cellar protruding from the hillside should be double-boarded or in some way protected against summer heat and winter cold.

We have never had to dig an outside root cellar, as we have been lucky enough to have cool-enough, warm-enough cellars. But all storehouses must be proof against invading rodents such as rats, mice, squirrels, raccoons and skunks.

We will never forget one of our winters in Maine when we had stored twelve bushels of apples in the cellar, supposed to be rat- and mouseproof. The apples were layered with abundant semidry autumn leaves below and above the fruit. We closed the door of the cellar and went off on a transcontinental lecture tour. On our return, four months later, we went down to the cellar to look over our dozen boxes of carefully stored apples. The floor was covered with leaves, inches deep. We felt in the boxes. Of the hundreds of stored apples only one apple remained—a fine specimen of Northern Spy. We never saw the marauder (probably a rat or a squirrel) nor could we find out where it got in and out. It had gone from box to box chewing up the apples and leaving some of the chewed pulp, the leaves, and one lone apple as a token for us latecomers. What a fine winter the animal must have had!

We take our beets, carrots, onions, garlic, turnips, rutabagas from the ground in the fall when they are mature. We dig them out, cutting off the green an inch or so from the top of the roots so they will not bleed. We store them in our root cellar in open boxes or baskets lined with dry leaves. We alternate layers of vegetables and leaves, no root touching another, so that if one root rots it will not affect its neighbors. We do the same with potatoes and apples. They will all keep fresh and crisp to the next harvest time. Periodically during the winter we go over the boxes (perhaps once a month) using up first those roots that show evidence of early deterioration.

The best temperature for storing in this open-boxed way is forty to forty-five degrees Fahrenheit. A centrally heated basement with a furnace in the cellar is too warm. No vegetable or fruit or canned produce has ever frozen in our forty-five-degree cellar. Freezing and thawing is what breaks the cells in plants or fruits. An even temperature allows plants and roots to survive in garden or house cellar or root cellar. The object is to keep them as "live" as possible for as long as possible.

Squash and pumpkin do not last as long as the root crops, but we can keep them (on wooden shelves or in baskets or boxes) into the New Year. Tomatoes and green peppers we keep in open boxes or baskets until Christmas; these are not stored in leaves. We have never found a good way of keeping cabbage, cauliflower and celery beyond the end of the year.

We have tried storing our root vegetables in sawdust and in sand, and prefer our leaf treatment. We gather the leaves in early fall, when they drop from the trees, push them into old maple-sap buckets we have kept from Vermont sugaring days, and keep two or three dozen pails in the cellar till we find time to put the roots to bed for the winter.

We feel that storing, processing or preserving foods is a poor alternative at best to the raw fresh thing. But choosing to live in New England with its delightful procession of the seasons, we take the bitter with the sweet, and the cold with the balmy. We had to work out some way to preserve our "cold weather vegetables" through the long winters.

There are four ways to keep spring, summer and fall garden produce: we can store as above described, in leaves; we can dry certain produce; we can preserve in glass jars; and we can freeze produce. Drying involves the least work and has other real benefits.

Although leaf vegetables only contain about 2 percent of protein, it is worth pointing out—and this is often overlooked—that the dry matter of such vegetables contains more than 20 percent protein. PYKE MAGNUS, *Man and Food*, 1970

Dried products do not require expensive containers, and they can be stored almost indefinitely, under proper conditions, in relatively small space. One hundred pounds of fresh vegetables may be reduced to an average of ten pounds by drying. Drying does not seem to injure the nutritive value of foods. HENRY GARY, *A Manual of Home-Making*, 1922

Peas and beans we leave to dry in their pods on the plants in the garden, and then we store them, shelled, in bottles or tins on the pantry shelf. These are used for winter suppers or as the base for year-round soups.

We have dried blueberries on cheese-clothed trays, put in the sun for two days, then into a very low oven till really dry. We have kept these berries in a cloth sack and when soaked have used as raisins.

Cranberries can be dried a little in the sun, then put into sterile dry bottles with tight covers. They will keep thus for years. An old recipe I read said that "cranberries will keep all winter in a firkin of water in the cellar." This we have never tried.

Pumpkin or squash can be dried by peeling and cutting into thin strips or slices. Spread out on a screen, they can dry in the sun, or in or over a moderate oven. Store in cloth bags in mouseproof containers. When wanted, soak overnight in cold water and cook the next day till tender in the same soak-water.

Apples can be cored, sliced and hung on strings in a warm kitchen. We also dry our herbs by hanging them in branches from the kitchen timbers, and strip them when wanted for teas or cooking. The herbs we dry in this way are parsley, celery leaves, dill, tarragon, basil, thyme, oregano, sage, summer savory, rosemary, hyssop, and many mints.

Our rose hips are the fruit of the Rosa Rugosa, which we found growing on the coast of Maine. We have cultivated the bushes until they now grow five or six feet tall and produce inch-size pods in the fall after the roses have bloomed.

To dry, gather when the hips are bright red-orange and still firm to the touch. Cut hips in half and dig out seeds with a knife or pointed spoon. (This is a tedious job.

Have someone read aloud or play some music while at it.) Spread on a tray in a lukewarm oven or on top of a warm stove. When thoroughly dry, put in an earthenware container or cloth sack and keep in a dry cool place. They can be pulverized and the powder used in teas or soups. (I also cut citrus rinds in strips, dry in a low oven and pulverize for teas or fruit soups.)

Even rhubarb can be dried!

> Rhubarb, when well-prepared, will keep good for an indefinite period. The stalks should be cut into pieces about an inch in length. These pieces should then be strung on a thin twine, and hung up to dry. Rhubarb shrinks in drying more than any other plant, and when dry strongly resembles pieces of soft wood. When wanted for use it should be soaked in water all night, and the next day stewed over a slow fire. SOLON ROBINSON, *Facts for Farmers,* 1869

I have not tried this way of drying rhubarb, but I have canned rhubarb cold and uncooked. I cut the stalks into two-inch pieces and pack them tightly into a sterilized but cold jar, filling it to overflowing with cold water. Seal tight and put in cellar. This will keep at least a year. Sweeten when serving. I won't say it's as good as fresh rhubarb!

Following are old-time recipes for drying plums, cherries, pumpkins, and tomatoes.

> The most kindely way to dry all manner of plums or Cherries in the Sunne: If it be a small fruite, you must dry them whole, by laying them abroad in the hote Sunne, in stone or pewter dishes, or iron or brasse pans, turning them as you shall see cause. But if the plum be of any largnesse, then give eyther plum a slit on each side; and if the Sunne does not shine sufficiently during the practice, then dry them in an Oven that is temperately warm. SIR HUGH PLATT, *Delightes for Ladies,* 1602

Pumpions are prepared for eating in various ways. The Indians boil them whole, or roast them in ashes. The French and English slice them, and put the slices before the fire to roast; when they are roasted, they generally put sugar on the pulp. . . . The Indians, in order to preserve the Pumpions for a very long time, cut them in long slices, which they fasten or twist together, and dry them either by the sun, or by the fire in a room. When they are thus dried, they will keep for years together, and when boiled, they taste very well. The Indians prepare them thus at home and on their journies and from them the Europeans have adopted this method.   PETER KALM,
Travels into North America, 1771

Scald, peel and stew tomatoes. Then spread on earthen plates and dry in sunshine or in a slow oven. It will resemble the pulp of dried peaches. When wanted for use in winter, soak a quantity in cold water and let soak up on back of stove. Sweetened, it is an excellent and cheap sauce.   SOLON ROBINSON,
Facts for Farmers, 1866

On our pantry shelves many staples are stored: raisins and prunes and nuts; grains such as wheat berries, rolled oats, rye, millet, barley, buckwheat, bran, alfalfa, rice, lentils, mung beans, popcorn, in small wooden barrels; sunflower seeds, pumpkin seeds and sesame in cans; bottles or cans of safflower, peanut and olive oils; maple syrup, honey, molasses; vinegar; peanut butter; seaweed. It constitutes a veritable health food store.

The shelves in our cellar are filled with around five hundred quart jars of applesauce, rose hip nectar and raspberry juice, soup stock, tomato juice.

With the coming of the so-called "self-sealing" glass fruit jars every pioneer family sought to can a quantity of fruit each season. These jars were too expensive, however, for the average frontier householder to be able to afford more than a few dozen at most. It is an interesting commentary on the size of pioneer families that every frontier housewife insisted upon half-gallon

jars, asserting that the quart size did not hold enough to go more than half way around in serving her family. Yet, the modern housewife virtually always demands either pint or quart jars, usually the former, and the half-gallon size has almost disappeared from the market.　　　　EDWARD EVERETT DALE,
The Food of the Frontier, 1947

Whatever vegetables or fruit I put up is done the open-kettle way—not processed in a hot water bath. The latter is more trouble and takes more time and I have never lost jars through souring or molding unless I had used an old rubber for sealing or an imperfect jar or cover.

To can applesauce I start the operation by filling the inside of a hot oven with clean quart jars from the cellar. They heat and sterilize while I prepare the sauce, cutting the apples into quarters, leaving on the skins but eliminating cores and any bad spots. Toss into cold water to wash. Put in kettles with minimum water. Cover. Cook till tender. Take a quart bottle out of the oven, set it on wooden board or dry cloth. To prevent jar from cracking when the hot apples are poured in, stand a long silver knife or spoon in the hot jar to act as conductor of the heat. Spoon the boiling hot apples from the first kettle into the jar, working down the jar with the knife to fill in any air bubbles. Fill right to the top. Cover with a tight seal, and bottle the next kettle full of sauce. When bottles cool, store in cellar. Sweeten to taste when serving.

Fruit juices and rose hip nectar are prepared in much the same way. Heat jars in oven. Fill each jar one-third full with boiling water, remembering to insert the metal knife before pouring in the hot water. Add a big tablespoon of honey, dissolving it by stirring. Drop in a cup and a half of fruit (blueberries, rose hips, blackberries, grapes, strawberries, raspberries). Fill jar to top with boiling water. Screw cover on tight and store away. Under the best conditions (with no interruptions and everything at hand) Scott and I can put up twenty quart jars in thirty minutes when we work at it together: he at the stove, keeping containers of water boiling and bringing me the jars, covers, rubbers and water.

We find that these bottled fruit juices keep indefinitely in the cool cellar. Some of them (especially the rose hips) seem to mature and have a better flavor in the second or third year. In any case, they do not deteriorate in that time. The juice from the rose hip bottles has such a delicate flavor I call it "faery food" and serve it in tiny, two-inch glasses as a liqueur. I gave it one time to an old Maine neighbor friend, who swigged it down and said, "Umph. Ain't got much kick, 'as it?" Well, the kick is in the vitamin C it contains—many times as much as fresh citrus juice.

We drink our homemade rose hip juice, slightly diluted, every morning at breakfast. The hips that are left in the bottle we store in the refrigerator till we have a quart or two. We whirl these in the blender with a minimum of water, put them through a sieve, using the resulting purée as a base for rose hip soups. The thick seedy remainder we drop in spoonfuls onto pie plates or cookie sheets and dry on the back of the stove. When crumbly we add this to our herb teas.

I do not bottle corn or beans, as they are the most difficult to keep even if pressure-cooked; although corn canned with an equal amount of tomatoes is fairly foolproof.

Soup stock and tomato juice I make thusly. Clean and quarter tomatoes, not peeling. (I put up almost a bushel at a time.) Fill your biggest kettles with the tomatoes, adding *no* water. Let the tomatoes cook down while you clean and chop up two or three bunches of celery, using all stalks but the heart (which I save for salad) and any leaves that are too tough and old. Peel and chop a dozen onions and great handfuls of parsley and some green peppers if you have them. Add these to your by-now cooked-down tomatoes. Boil moderately until the celery (your toughest item) is forkable. When done, strain off the liquid, setting aside the solid part for later. Heat the liquid to boiling again, adding a small bundle of assorted fresh herbs which you fish out before bottling. Ladle the boiling tomato juice into hot sterilized jars (remembering to put in a silver knife to conduct the heat), fill to tip-top, seal, cool and put away.

The thick residue should now be reheated in kettles with a minimum of water added, to prevent scorching. As soon as it boils in one kettle, fill jar, knifing down to prevent air bubbles. Halfway through the bottle add a teaspoon of sea salt, then continue filling to top. Seal. Continue the process, kettle after kettle, till all thick material is used up. This thick stock, as well as the liquid, is handy for soups throughout the year.

A friend, Madith Smith, sent me her recipe for tomato soup stock which might be better than mine as it is less cooked, but one needs a blender. She heats a half bushel of tomatoes, unskinned, quartered, till soft, and strains off the juice (apparently not using the tomato residue). She then puts in a blender 4 chopped onions, 1 head chopped celery and 2 green peppers, adding 3 teaspoons of salt and 3 teaspoons sugar (!), with enough juice to churn. This mixture she adds to her plain tomato juice, which has been cooking. She boils it all together, then bottles.

My freezing requires no time charts. I freeze peas (young sugar peas in their pods or regular shelled peas) by dropping them into boiling water. When they begin to change color they are blanched enough and I lift them out or strain them through a sieve (keeping the liquid for the next batch of peas or for the next soup). I spread them out to cool or dip them into ice water, then pack them in bags or cartons and put them in the freezer. The same may be done with young green beans.

Here is a method of *no* blanching which works both with peas or green beans. Put raw in a freezer container (box or bag), cover with cold water, leaving space for expansion. Seal and freeze. When you're ready to eat the peas or beans, put the frozen block of vegetables in a pan and heat till piping hot.

Corn need not be blanched for freezing. Remove the husks and put directly into freezing bags, without any water or washing. To be eaten, put cobs in a shallow baking dish, spread with butter and bake in a hot oven for fifteen to twenty minutes.

Young zucchini squash can be put single-layered on pans and frozen in freezer, then transferred to bags or boxes and stored in freezer. To cook, chop into pieces and stir-fry in butter or oil with a few herbs. A fancier way for zucchini is to cut up the raw squash into half-inch chunks, and simmer with some ripe red tomatoes and some sliced onions. Add a few leaves of basil and sprigs of oregano. Cool and put in containers in freezer.

Frozen asparagus, when thawed and cooked, become limp and tasteless. I serve it straight from the freezer. If eaten by hand in the semifrozen stage, before the stems thaw, it is a delicious, unique icy hors d'oeuvre. Some guests have called it "asperge glacé."

Whole tomatoes (the small plum or cherry size) should

also be eaten before completely thawed. I pack jars full of the raw fruit and put them directly into the freezer. I also simmer large tomatoes, quartering them so that they will break up better, and ladle them into jars for freezing. These barely cooked tomatoes are indispensable for use in soups and stews.

Cucumber slices can be packed in pint jars and frozen with onion slices and vinegar. They also can be eaten semithawed.

Shell beans (green beans that have matured on the vines but not yet dried) I boil and cool and freeze in containers. They are one of our most useful staples for winter.

Quantities of parsley, chopped up with celery, onion and green pepper, is a pleasant thing to find when digging through the freezer in midwinter.

Strawberries and blueberries and cherries are the easiest of all to freeze. I don't even wash them if they come from our own place. I just pour them from the quart basket into cellophane bags or cardboard cartons and pack them away in the freezer. Peaches I peel and slice and stir up with a bit of maple syrup or honey and store in cottage cheese containers.

All so far mentioned has been indoor storage of fruits and vegetables. We also have a sun-heated greenhouse that stays green all winter with parsley, lettuces, leeks and carrots, rare additions to our menu in midwinter. The outside garden carries over, through the bitterest weather, kale, brussels sprouts and often spinach and other hardy greens, to the coming of spring. I can say we eat our own food year-round, with only intermittent excursions off the place to buy extras. The imported additions to our home food supply are nice but not necessary: citrus, avocados, nuts, raisins, dates, prunes. Most of these, along with oil, butter, cheese, and grains, we can order from our local co-op.

It goes without saying that if possible we prefer to grow all our own food and have it "garden fresh," but in our climate this is not feasible. We therefore have worked out these various ways to store, dry, freeze, can and otherwise preserve what foods are not eaten straight from the garden.

Our homegrown food enables us to live simply, frugally and healthfully what we call our Good Life. Scott and I have kept hale and hearty for more than half a century eating this way. It may be worth a try for you to more than scan these recipes of simple food for simple people.

> This little work would have been a treasure to herself when she first set out in life, and she therefore hopes it may prove useful to others. In that expectation it is given to the Public.
> A Lady, *A New System of Domestic Cookery Formed upon Principles of Economy,* 1812

Index

299